"Through their book *Removing the Sta.* [barcode] *ist Convention*, Jarvis Williams and Kevin J ~~Southern Baptists. The sin of racism universally plagues the human conscience and history bears testimony to the fact that Southern Baptists are by no means immune. Yet, what greater opportunity for the reconciling power of the gospel to be displayed than in a denomination birth marked with the sin of racism? Contributors to this work can seldom avoid referencing their personal stories, evidencing the extent to which the book reveals the souls of the authors. Rest assured, the chapters will also touch the souls of the readers. Southern Baptists have needed this book for a long time. Thank you, Jarvis Williams and Kevin Jones, for having the courage to provide it. Might it push us towards greater faithfulness in love and reconciliation."

—**Paul H. Chitwood**, executive director, Kentucky Baptist Convention

"*Removing the Stain of Racism* is not only essential reading for all who are committed to racial reconciliation in the SBC, but is a call to genuine repentance and gospel-centered living for Christ-followers everywhere. In so many ways, the book marks a moment of celebration for the sanctified progress that has been made in intercultural relations in recent years. On the other hand, the book sadly and starkly reminds readers of our fallenness and ongoing failures. Readers should reflect with care, doing so with an open Bible along with a prepared heart, recognizing the need for continued faithfulness, further illumination, and enhanced understanding. Jarvis Williams, Kevin Jones, and the contributors to this most-important volume are to be commended and congratulated for producing this bold and timely work."

—**David S. Dockery**, president, Trinity International University/Trinity Evangelical Divinity School

"In this important, beautifully edited volume, Jarvis J. Williams and Kevin Jones bring together a *tour de force* of authors and knowledge. The brilliance of this book is we are not simply told of a need to remove the stain of racism, we are shown how—biblically, theologically, ethically, pastorally, administratively, educationally, and much more. A true gift to the church—whether Southern Baptist or any other branch of the Christian faith—this is a must read for those serious about removing the deep stain of racism."

—**Michael O. Emerson**, provost, North Park University, and co-author of *Divided by Faith: Evangelical Religion and the Problem of Race in America*

"Topics ranging from biblical studies, to Southern Baptist history and theology, to educational philosophy and implementation, to contemporary analyses of race relations today, are all arrayed with prophetic voice to address the stain of racism. Though the focus is on the SBC, the writers bring this voice to the church of Jesus Christ in general. I applaud the expertise and courage of each contributor."

—**Bruce L. Fields**, professor of faith and culture, Trinity International University/Trinity Evangelical Divinity School

"In describing the existential dilemma of being both a Negro and an American in the 20th century, W.E.B. DuBois wrote the following: 'One ever feels his two-ness—an American, a Negro; two souls, two thoughts, two unreconciled strivings; two warring ideals in one dark body, whose dogged strength alone keeps it from being torn asunder.' Replace 'American' with 'Southern Baptist' and you arrive at what many, if not most, black evangelicals continue to experience in Southern Baptist life. This timely work unpacks this experience via personal narrative and gospel-centered expertise. Since its very inception, the Southern Baptist Convention has often served as exhibit A of the co-constituted nature of religion and race. From their respective sites of Convention service, contributors reckon with this history and its present impact, while considering important themes like white supremacy, racial bias, representation, power, privilege, paternalism, enduring notions of intellectual inferiority/superiority, etc. And while the authors are conversant with these thematics—given their usefulness for the purpose of analysis and diagnosis—they are clear that, at root, the fundamental problem is sin, and the ultimate remedy, the power of the gospel. Nevertheless, the stain of racism—in terms of the black/white binary in particular (and for legitimate reasons)—is rightly centered as a topic worthy of exclusive attention. No one considers it unorthodox to spray spot removal on a specific stain before placing the item in the washer. Likewise, no one avoids a stain in the hope that it will be removed by washing around it. No, we must not fear the conversation. Yes, racism is alive and at work in the SBC. But so is Jesus. This work deals honestly with the former and points us all to the hope inherent in the latter. Southern Baptists of every shade ought to take up and read!"

—**Steven Harris**, director of advocacy, The Ethics and Religious Liberty
Commission of the Southern Baptist Convention

"The stain of racism has been on our convention for far too long. As Southern Baptists, we've made great strides over the past two decades, yet our work is not done. Williams and Jones offer gospel-saturated biblical insights on how we can see Christ purge not only our convention but his global bride from every sinful implication of racism. I'm hopeful for the future of our cooperative work in mission together, and believe we can learn from *Removing the Stain of Racism* in such a way that we will reflect Christ's body as seen in Revelation 7:9."

—**D. A. Horton**, pastor, Reach Fellowship, North Long Beach, CA,
and chief evangelist, Urban Youth Workers Institute

"A stain of racism has marked the Southern Baptist Convention from the beginning—but this stain does not have to remain. The SBC has repeatedly declared a desire for a more diverse future, but this book does far more than merely make another declaration. In these pages, a diverse group of authors work together to plot a clear pathway toward a more colorful future. As a pastor in a multi-ethnic community and as a parent in a multi-racial household, my prayer is that God will use this book in such a way that a far more wondrous kaleidoscope of colors and cultures will mark the future of the SBC."

—**Timothy Paul Jones**, C. Edwin Gheens Professor of
Christian Family Ministry, The Southern Baptist Theological Seminary,
and preaching elder, Sojourn Community Church, Midtown Louisville

"*Removing the Stain of Racism from the Southern Baptist Convention*, edited by Drs. Jarvis J. Williams and Kevin M. Jones, is an important text that deals critically with the disastrous racial legacy of the Southern Baptist Convention that continues to bear devastating implications for interracial and interethnic Christian relations today, and the Christian project of racial unity and reconciliation in contemporary evangelical American churches. The authors of this volume categorically argue that racism is the antithesis of the gospel of reconciliation, which Christians are called to embody, practice, and live effectively in society. Not only has the book constructively established the historical causes of racism in the SBC, the authors have brilliantly articulated the moral, ethical, biblical, theological, and pastoral arguments or justifications to end 'the Sunday morning segregation' and to remove the racial vestiges in contemporary SBC churches and leadership. This book makes a clarion call to contemporary Southern Baptist Christians and evangelical churches in America to transcend the barriers of race, ethnicity, ideology, and cultural traditions for the sake of Christ, for the sake of the gospel, and for the sake of the lost—to the majestic glory and fame of the eternal and immortal Triune God. *Removing the Stain of Racism* is a must read for every Southern Baptist Christian, seminary professor, seminary student, seminary president, and all individuals in the SBC administration!"

—**Celucien L. Joseph**, assistant professor of English,
Indian River State College, and author of *Radical Humanism
and Generous Tolerance: Soyinka on Religion and Human Solidarity*

"Among all American denominations, the Southern Baptist Convention may have the heaviest burden to bear with regard to the history of racial injustice. Thus, it is heartening to see a volume like this one, which is brimming with judicious reflections and compelling exhortations on how we can break down the 'dividing walls of hostility' that still separate Baptists."

—**Thomas S. Kidd**, distinguished professor of history, Baylor University

"This honest, unveiling confrontation of the SBC's past is the foundation needed to bring about meaningful change in the present, and establish a renewed SBC in the future."

—**Alex Medina**, senior designer, Vox Media, and music producer for
Lecrae, Andy Mineo, and Trip Lee

"White supremacy and racial injustice are antichrist. The time is well past to end any hedging on the past horrors and the present challenges of the Southern Baptist Convention. The Southern Baptist Convention of the year 2050 will be truly multiethnic, or it will be dead. Which of these two paths is chosen will depend on how much gospel courage this generation will have, and on how much we believe the inerrant Bible we preach. May God use *Removing the Stain* to help us!"

—**Russell D. Moore**, president, The Ethics and Religious Liberty
Commission of the Southern Baptist Convention

"In social and political terms, racial discrimination has been the United States' original sin. This powerful book is written for Southern Baptists, but should be read by all American believers. It overflows with pastoral, historical, denominational, theological, cultural, and especially biblical wisdom. It is also ideally organized for use by congregations and classes in college and seminary. Its great strength is to root the hope of racial reconciliation in the promise of the gospel."

—**Mark Noll**, Francis A. McAnaney Professor of History,
University of Notre Dame, and author of
God and Race in American Politics: A Short History

"When it comes to the deep wounds of racism in the SBC, the bandages that have been used to stop the bleeding won't work. Nothing short of a scalpel in the hands of a skilled physician will do. That's what this book is and that's what it does. Each chapter is written by a skilled physician addressing the issue of racism from their area of expertise. It cuts deep, in order to bring real healing. It's brutally honest about things that have been ignored, denied, and unaddressed for so long. But it doesn't stop there. The aim of this book isn't lament, but lasting change. But the pathway to lasting change is paved with stones of discomfort that come from honest dialogue. I'm eager to see how the Lord uses this in the life of pastors, churches, and this denomination."

—**John Onwuchekwa**, lead pastor, Cornerstone Church, Atlanta, GA

"Wherever the gospel goes in divine power, humility and courage beautify God's people. *Removing the Stain of Racism* stands as an unmistakable evidence of gospel power moving through the Southern Baptist Convention in these momentous days. May this timely book encourage all believers toward such humility and courage that this generation might see the beauty of Jesus among us."

—**Ray Ortlund**, lead pastor, Immanuel, Nashville, TN

"God spoke the last word at the very first. 'Eve is the mother of all living' (Genesis 3:20 NKJV). Racism is an expression of the innate evil in the heart of men. This book, edited by Jarvis Williams and Kevin Jones, is brain and heart surgery for all Southern Baptists. The volume is a compass to assist us in finding our way from the labyrinth of iniquity in which many of our founders languished, and in which all too many still remain. If you care, read this book. If you do not care, there is yet time to repent."

—**Paige Patterson**, president, Southwestern Baptist Theological Seminary

"Contributors to *Removing the Stain* write with love for Christ and his body, and express that love with great clarity, passion, and practicality. This work is much needed for a church culture fatigued with discussions on race and racism, yet still miles from the Christian unity, diversity, integration, and reconciliation the New Testament exhorts God's people to embrace. May many inside and outside of the SBC read this team's work and so strive to help move their congregations toward the removal of remaining spots, blind spots, and blemishes related to racism, for the sake of Christ's glory in all the earth."

—**Eric C. Redmond**, assistant professor of Bible, Moody Bible Institute, and associate pastor of adult ministries, Calvary Memorial Church, Oak Park, IL

"*Removing the Stain of Racism* is an important book! It's important because it forces Southern Baptists to take an honest look back at an origin that is directly linked with a defense of slavery. It's an important book because it also forces Southern Baptists to look forward with humility, knowing that the sins of the past, if forgotten, can easily become, once again, the sins of the future. Finally, it's an important book because it reminds us that the God who gave us a Jewish savior from the seed of a traitorous prostitute (Rahab), a murdering adulterer (David), and a promiscuous head of state (Solomon), is also the God who offers hope and forgiveness to all repentant sinners, including repentant racists, be they individuals or institutions. If you doubt there is a stain of racism in the Southern Baptist Convention, I challenge you to read this book and learn from it. If you want to be a part of the much-needed change for the better in the Southern Baptist Convention, I encourage you to read this book, and, by God's grace and in his strength, join in the work to remove this stain."

—**Juan R. Sanchez**, senior pastor, High Pointe Baptist Church, Austin, TX

"This collection, *Removing the Stain of Racism from the Southern Baptist Convention*, seeks to lance the boil of racism and drain its unhealthy and sinister content instead of simply providing a band aid for a wound that will not heal on its own. These essays espouse that believers in the Southern Baptist Convention can and must exhibit *unity* without seeking a false optimism of *uniformity*. The way to reconciliation is through *Christoconciliation*—unity in Christ in the midst of diversity. Those who have ears to hear let them hear what the writers and editors, Jarvis Williams and Kevin Jones, are saying to the churches of the Southern Baptist Convention."

—**Robert Smith Jr.**, Charles T. Carter Baptist Chair of Divinity, Beeson Divinity School/Samford University

"The editors of and contributors to *Removing the Stain of Racism* model, through writing, the kind of leadership the church needs to practice in the 21st century—one that places more racial minorities at the forefront. These pastors, scholars, and administrators speak the cutting truth about racism in the nation's largest Protestant denomination but do so with a profound love for Christ's church that is evident in both the critiques and the encouragements they offer. This book will shine as a lamp of reconciliation for generations to come and gives other Christian denominations, fellowships, and institutions an example to follow. Praise the Lord for progress!"

—**Jemar Tisby**, president and co-founder, Reformed African American Network, and co-host of Pass the Mic podcast

"This courageous resource is a major contribution to the Body of Christ. The editors, Kevin Jones and Jarvis Williams, do a spectacular job producing a project that prophetically speaks to the obstacles and opportunities of racial reconciliation in the Southern Baptist Convention. Each chapter will be an encouragement and a challenge. I highly doubt readers will walk away from this book the same. When it comes to racial harmony the authors are bold, passionate, winsome, and gospel-centered. I pray that their tribe increases in our denomination and in the Kingdom abroad."

—**Cam Triggs**, lead pastor, Grace Alive, Orlando, FL

"Social ethics in general and racism in particular have for far too long prevented the Bible-believing church from being a credible witness to broader American society. And so there is a great need for a movement of repentance and reconciliation in the American church that recovers the Bible's social ethical framework, connecting it to God's redemptive purposes in the gospel. *Removing the Stain of Racism from the Southern Baptist Convention* is a serious motion in that broader movement. The diverse group of writers contributing to the book not only bring biblical light in examining the sins of the SBC's past, but each also takes care to own the SBC's failures as their responsibility, even across ethnic and cultural differences. Compellingly, the book's focus is to overcome the ills of racism in the concrete reality of a specific situation, the social and spiritual life of the Southern Baptist Convention and its churches. Written with the force and weight reminiscent of Soong-Chan Rah's *The Next Evangelicalism*, this book should not only be read by pastors and leaders, but should be studied and used as a reference by churches and other gospel movements in their own particular pursuits of racial reconciliation."

—**Darryl Williamson**, lead pastor, Living Faith Bible Fellowship, Tampa, FL

"*Removing the Stain of Racism* comes at a critical time in the history of the SBC and in the life of the nation. With acute wisdom, piercing personal reflection, expert and honest historical assessment, and mature scriptural and theological analysis, the contributors have offered a most insightful and practical guide for people of all races to take meaningful steps toward fruit-bearing repentance and biblical reconciliation. This book is practically and intellectually indispensable for Baptists, and Christians from every denomination, as we face up to our individual and corporate responsibilities toward one another."

—**John D. Wilsey**, assistant professor of history and Christian apologetics, and associate director, Land Center for Cultural Engagement, Southwestern Baptist Theological Seminary

REMOVING THE STAIN OF RACISM

FROM THE SOUTHERN BAPTIST CONVENTION

REMOVING
THE STAIN OF
RACISM

FROM THE SOUTHERN BAPTIST CONVENTION

JARVIS J. WILLIAMS *and* KEVIN M. JONES

DIVERSE AFRICAN AMERICAN AND WHITE PERSPECTIVES

ACADEMIC

NASHVILLE, TENNESSEE

Kevin dedicates this book to
Kennedi, Kevin Jr., and Karsynn, my beloved children whom I pray
will be a part of an SBC where the stain of racism no longer exists.

Jarvis dedicates this book to Brother Mike and to the saints at
Hindman First Baptist Church for their labor of love to remove
the stain of racism from the SBC.

CONTENTS

FOREWORD

K. MARSHALL WILLIAMS SR.

We are living in a sin-sick, self-centered, secular society that is filled with greed, anger, hostility, hatred, racism, and injustice. America's current racial strife (from Ferguson to Cleveland) makes this apparent. Time is winding down, sin is running rampant, and people are falling away from the Christian faith. These are the last and evil days, filled with satanic activity. Judgment is coming. Our world is lost and in need of our Savior, the Lord Jesus who is the Christ, the Son of the true and living God!

Historically the root causes of racism in the Southern Baptist Convention are sin and white supremacist ideology, mixed with the false interpretation of Scripture, including teachings of the so-called curse of Ham (Gen 9:24–25). The fact that the stain still exists in the SBC is evidence of unrepentant, fallen humanity that has been shaped in iniquity. The stain still exists because we are in a spiritual battle. We are not wrestling against flesh and blood but against satanic strongholds that entice the flesh and get embedded in the DNA of sinner and saint alike in our world (Eph 6:10–18).

As children of the Most High God and overcomers in Christ, we need to remember two things to eradicate the stain of racism. First, we have the Almighty's power and authority (Matt 28:18) and the power of the Spirit (Rom 8:9), who lives in every believer (John 16:7–13; Acts 1:8; Rom 8:9).

The Lord has bestowed upon us everything that we need to live godly lives (2 Pet 1:3–4). As Christians, we need to be filled with and controlled by the Spirit, not walking in the lusts of the flesh, so that we can produce the fruit of the Spirit (Matt 3:8; Gal 5:16; Eph 5:18; Phil 4:6–7). A few examples of this Spirit-empowered fruit are love, joy, peace, patience, kindness, gentleness, self-control, and avoidance of all fleshly lusts (Gal 5:16–22). If we walk in the Spirit, produce the fruit of repentance, and absolutely trust in God's sovereign power to enable us to pursue horizontal love with those from different races in the SBC and beyond, then we will see reconciliation among all ethnicities as we live in community with one another as a sanctified people of God (2 Cor 7:1; Gal 2:20; Heb 12:14).

The Almighty's power is sufficient to save the nations from their sins and from God's wrath (Eph 2:1–10), but it can also overrule the stains of systemic racial injustice and oppression, economic and educational inequalities, and the new Jim Crowism, the pipeline from school to prison. Because the God of Southern Baptists from every racial stripe is the God and Father of our Jewish Lord and Savior Jesus Christ, our God is able to do exceedingly, abundantly above all we can ask or think (Eph 3:20–21).

In 1995 the SBC "unwaveringly denounced racism, in all its forms, as deplorable sin," and affirmed "every human life as sacred . . . of equal and immeasurable worth, made in God's image, regardless of race or ethnicity."[1] Today I want the SBC to put its racial reconciliation money where its racial reconciliation resolution is. As an African-American Southern Baptist pastor, I am personally putting some flesh on that resolution by calling the body of Christ in the SBC to a Great Commandment revival. Matthew 22:37–40 says that inextricably linked to loving God is loving people. The SBC has

---

[1] "Resolution on Racial Reconciliation on the 150th Anniversary of the Southern Baptist Convention," Southern Baptist Convention, 1995, accessed July 16, 2016, http://www.sbc.net/resolutions/899/resolution-on-racial-reconciliation-on-the-150th-anniversary-of-the-southern-baptist-convention.

always had a heart for the edification of the saints and the evangelization of the sinner. That is the Great Commission (Matt 28:19–20). But without strict adherence to the Great Commandment, we have no mission.

My ability to be in a right horizontal relationship with my neighbor is inextricably linked to my vertical relationship with the Lord (John 15:5; Rom 5:1; Eph 2:11–3:8)—a point too many Southern Baptists have verbally acknowledged but practically failed to work out. For example, just read the SBC resolutions on race relations from 1845 to the 1900s and compare the numerous positive statements about treating African-Americans in a respectful and dignified way with what many Southern Baptists actually did to terrorize African-Americans simply because their bodies were not white.

Apart from regeneration no one has the capacity to be in right relationship with his neighbor (Rom 7:18; 14–15; Eph 4–5). Christians from every tongue, tribe, people, and nation are agents of reconciliation and ambassadors for Christ (2 Cor 5:18–20). Christians should be living epistles read by all men (2 Cor 3:2). Christians are the light of the world and the salt of the earth (Matt 5:14–16; John 8:12). A godly Christian life is a strong (and maybe a convincing) testimony that Jesus is alive, the power of God is real, and the Bible is the Word of God (Matt 5:16; John 8:36; 11:25–26; 1 Cor 11:1; 2 Cor 5:17; Heb 4:11–12).

Every race of man needs to see Christians live out their faith so that when we stand up to preach the reconciling power of the gospel to them, they will have reasons in advance to hear it and respond to it by faith (Ps 51:10–13; Matt 7:1–5; 1 Cor 9:24–27). They need to hear the Word preached, but they need to see the Word lived out in faithful, Spirit-empowered obedience (Jas 1:19–27). Obeying the Great Commandment of love will lead to authentic Christian living and inexplicable unity among all races that may, if God wills, usher a revival of racial reconciliation into the church. I hear the minor prophet Micah's words echoing down the corridors of time: "to act justly, to love faithfulness, and to walk humbly with your God" (Mic 6:8).

Many have already given their lives for the longstanding cry for justice and equality in America. As blood-bought believers who have been birthed into the body of Christ, we are being summoned by God to be kingdom citizens, not elevating our political ideologies or our cultural ethnicities over our biblical authenticity (Matt 6:33; 16:24–25; Rom 12:1–2; 1 Cor 6:19–20; 2 Cor 5:17; 1 Tim 2:4; 1 Pet 2:9). The call today is for us not to be pimps or puppets but prophets who will speak truth to power and exclaim like Amos, "Let justice flow like water, and righteousness, like an unfailing stream" (Amos 5:24)!

May my Southern Baptist brothers and sisters throughout the world recognize that we are all from one blood, one race (Gen 3:20; Acts 17:26). We are created by God for God's glory (Gen 3:20; Acts 17:26; Isa 43:7). Let us rise up and be a people whose God truly is the Lord. Let us choose this day whom we are going to serve (Josh 24:15). May God our Father, Jesus Christ our Lord, and the Holy Spirit our Comforter use this book to help all Southern Baptists from every tongue, tribe, people, and nation discover their roles in helping to remove the stain of racism from the SBC.

PREFACE

Who likes stains? Nothing is worse than having a clean, white shirt stained by a foreign substance. You might find yourself frantically rushing to the restroom, or fumbling through a purse looking for a life-saving bleach pin, or saturating a shirt in the evening with some form of concentrated cleaner to remove the stain. Maybe dry cleaning could help. Sometimes stains are quickly removed. On other occasions, stains must be treated with multiple applications. Frustrated with the process of removing the stain, you might throw away the shirt because stains have been known to ruin perfectly nice shirts.

But would you give up your efforts to remove the stain from a cherished shirt? If you truly cherished it, the answer would be no! In all likelihood you would treat the shirt until the stain was removed.

The Southern Baptist Convention has a big, dark, historical stain on it: racism. Evident by the SBC's affirmation of slavery, its failure to repudiate this sin until 1995, and the numerous segregated Southern Baptist churches, this stain continues to hinder Southern Baptist churches from embracing the one new man in Christ outlined in Ephesians 2:11–22 and from participating in the new song of those saints from every tongue, tribe, people, and nation referenced in Revelation 5:9. The gospel of Jesus Christ requires and demands all Southern Baptists to do their parts to erase this stain from the SBC—or at least to make the stain less apparent. This act requires a relentless commitment to Christian unity. And Christian unity requires us as a denomination to make the necessary sacrifices and to take the necessary steps to experience this unity in every aspect of Southern Baptist life sooner rather than later. This book, edited by and written primarily by African-American voices in the SBC, is one small effort to help erase the stain of racism from the SBC in pursuit of unity in our beloved denomination.

Why This Book?

Since African-Americans and white Southern Baptists have historically had a complicated and messy relationship in the United States and since African-Americans are usually not the denomination's primary spokespersons, we wanted to compile a book using predominately African-American contributors (young and old) from various aspects of SBC life: academic, administration, curriculum development, pastoral ministry, and state convention leadership. However, since removing the stain of racism in the SBC requires multiracial partnerships between both the majority group and all minority groups within the SBC and since we believe the white majority within the SBC has a unique responsibility to share leadership and influence with African-Americans in particular and all ethnic minorities in general, we wanted to include at least three voices from the white majority group. The three white contributors are Daniel L. Akin (president of Southeastern Baptist Theological Seminary), Matthew J. Hall (Dean of Boyce College at The Southern Baptist Theological Seminary), and R. Albert Mohler Jr. (president of The Southern Baptist Theological Seminary). These men are committed to this issue at a national level in the SBC and within two of our convention's seminaries.

The editors inclusion of white Southern Baptists alongside a majority of African-American contributors symbolizes the kind of partnership we as African-American editors believe must take place within the SBC if the stain of racism is to be removed once and for all. The historical stain of racism in the SBC exists in part because of the participation of many white Southern Baptists in the marginalization, oppression, and exploitation of black and brown people. As editors, we do not believe racism necessarily will be removed if more black and brown Southern Baptists are in leadership over the white majority in the SBC. Neither do we believe racial discrimination is a sin committed only by the white majority. Black and brown people discriminate, too! We mean the ethnic status quo in the SBC, which has historically privileged the white majority over black and brown people, can no longer remain the status quo if the stain of racism is to be removed from the SBC. A book edited by African-American Southern Baptists, with a majority of African-American contributors and only three contributions from the majority group represents the kind of partnership we think must take place within the SBC if the stain of racism is to be removed from the denomination.

Furthermore, we recognize that Southern Baptists come in many different shapes, sizes, ages, and colors. Both we and the contributors are well aware of both our country's and our denomination's increasing Latino/Hispanic population (Jarvis's wife is a Latina!). Thus, the emphasis on the black versus white divide in this book is not intended to communicate that the stain of racism in the SBC relates only to the black versus white divide. We simply understand that historically this is a significant reason for the existence of the SBC. Southern Baptists were a pro-slavery group. Many white Southern Baptists historically committed acts of terrorism against African-Americans because of their belief in and commitment to white supremacy, and many Southern Baptists from diverse races continue to benefit from the white majority's historic exploitation and marginalization of black and brown bodies.

We think a book like this, edited by African-American Southern Baptists and written predominantly by African-American Southern Baptists with invited contributions from white Southern Baptists, sends a powerful symbolic message. If the stain of racism is to be removed, the white majority must be willing to partner with and submit lovingly and humbly to the leadership of their vetted, qualified, and gifted black and brown brothers and sisters in the SBC. There needs to be a book with contributors representing every ethnic demographic in the SBC. But we hope readers from other minority groups will understand why we have focused on the black-and-white divide and will forgive us in advance for any wounds we might cause by not including more diverse voices.

ACKNOWLEDGMENTS

We have many people to thank for the completion of this book. We offer many thanks to Jim Baird, his team, and the entire B&H Academic family. When we presented this book to Jim and his team via a conference call in the spring of 2015, they immediately embraced the concept and offered helpful comments that have made the final product so much better than it would have otherwise been. Jim's commitment to reconciliation and his eager willingness to publish books on matters related to race and reconciliation by conservative African-American authors is a breath of fresh air in an age in which many books are coming off conservative evangelical presses written by white men.

We offer many thanks to every contributor and every endorser. We especially thank the contributors for telling their stories in an honest and raw way, using the Bible as their guide and Southern Baptist pastors, churches, and leaders as their audience. Each contributor sacrificed time from his own ministry or scholarship to write his essay. K. Marshall Williams Sr. wrote the foreword. R. Albert Mohler Jr. wrote chapter 1 ("Conceived in Sin, Called by the Gospel: The Root Cause of the Stain of Racism in the Southern Baptist Convention"). Matthew J. Hall wrote chapter 2 ("Historical Causes of the Stain of Racism in the Southern Baptist Convention"). Jarvis J. Williams wrote chapter 3 ("Biblical Steps Toward Removing the Stain of Racism from the Southern Baptist Convention"). Walter R. Strictland II wrote chapter 4

("Theological Steps Toward Removing the Stain of Racism from the Southern Baptist Convention"). Craig Mitchell wrote chapter 5 ("The Role of Ethics in Removing the Stain of Racism from the Southern Baptist Convention"). Kevin L. Smith wrote chapter 6 ("'Play the Men': Preaching and Pastoral Steps Toward Removing the Stain of Racism from the Southern Baptist Convention"). Mark A. Croston Sr. wrote chapter 7 ("Administrative Steps Toward Removing the Stain of Racism from the Southern Baptist Convention"). Kevin M. Jones Sr. wrote chapter 8 ("Educational Steps Toward Removing the Stain of Racism from the Southern Baptist Convention"). Toby Jennings wrote chapter 9 ("Publishing for Church Leaders to Remove the Stain of Racism from the Southern Baptist Convention"). With short notice and quick turnaround, Curtis A. Woods wrote chapter 10 ("Are We There Yet? Concluding Thoughts About Removing the Stain of Racism from the Southern Baptist Convention").

W. Dwight McKissic Sr. wrote epilogue 1 ("Why the Stain of Racism Remains in the Southern Baptist Convention: An African-American Pastor's Perspective"). Daniel L. Akin wrote epilogue 2 ("Why the Stain of Racism Remains in the Southern Baptist Convention: An Anglo Seminary President's Perspective"). T. Vaughn Walker wrote a heartfelt postscript. Walker was the first African-American faculty member to be hired at any SBC seminary.

Kevin Jones also compiled two appendices. The first lists a plethora of books and articles written by ethnically diverse authors on race, racism, and reconciliation. The second appendix provides a sample syllabus to give educators within the SBC an idea of how to teach on issues related to race, racism, and reconciliation in the convention. Authors and editors know by personal experience the sacrifices that go into writing anything. Thus, we as editors and authors are thankful for each contributor's labor and for trusting us to edit their work on the important issues of race, racism, and reconciliation within the SBC.

We offer many thanks to the various conferences, academic venues, and churches in which the information in this book has been preached and taught throughout the country. We also thank all of our students of various ethnicities at Boyce College and Southern Seminary who are increasingly engaging one another and their professors on matters related to race and racism. There are far too many students to thank by name, but all of our students should know they have contributed to this work in more ways than either they or we are consciously aware by probing us with difficult questions about the topics herein.

We offer many thanks to our families and friends. Kevin is thankful for Demica, his wife of twelve years, and their children. He is especially thankful for her belief in and support of the book. We are also thankful for numerous friends who have expressed interest in the book, in the work of reconciliation, and/or who have encouraged us in the cause of reconciliation in one way or another. There are too many to mention, but a few are Anna and Cody Farthing, Joseph Dicks, Matthew J. Hall, Andrew King, Timothy Kleiser, Evan Calvin, Nate Bishop, Abigail Cavanaugh, Rynetta Davis, Curtis Woods, and Valerie Patton. Their insights, friendship, and encouragement have made this book better.

Jarvis is especially thankful for his wife of fourteen years, Ana, and his seven-year-old son, Jaden. With each book he has written, his family has given much support and has made many sacrifices. Besides Jesus, they are certainly the most important people in his life. Their sacrifices are not always rewarded on earth but are always appreciated!

We hope this book serves our colorful and diverse SBC family, especially our churches, like a potent stain remover. Although we are fully aware Southern Baptists cannot change their racist past, our prayer is that the book will help Southern Baptists erase the stain of racism from our denomination's present, will direct its future, and will deal with an issue that still prohibits us from achieving Christian unity in the denomination. At the very least we pray that this book will make Southern Baptists aware of the stain of racism, that it will make them aware that Southern Baptists historically have been part of the problem and solution, and that it will give Southern Baptists ideas of how they can work together to become part of the solution of removing and keeping the stain of racism out of SBC life.

Finally, we dedicate this book to Kennedi, Kevin Jr., and Karsynn, and to Brother Mike Caudill (pastor of the Hindman First Baptist Church). As readers will see from Jarvis's chapter, from 1996 to 2000 Brother Mike and the saints at Hindman First Baptist Church had a tremendous impact on his life. He became the first African-American member of this Southern Baptist church in a part of eastern Kentucky that has historically had its fair share of race-related problems. Yet under Brother Mike's leadership, this small church personified reconciliation by embracing him into their family of faith when he was converted, by licensing him into the gospel ministry, by ordaining him into it, by ministering to his physical and spiritual needs, and by giving him many opportunities to exercise his gifts of preaching and teaching as he sought to discern his calling into ministry. Moreover, Brother Mike boldly preached against racism from the pulpit and personally poured his life into Jarvis by giving of his time and personal resources (especially books!) to nourish him in the faith. Thus, with much gratitude and great joy, Jarvis dedicates this book to Brother Mike and to the saints at Hindman First Baptist Church for their labor of love to remove the stain of racism from the SBC ministry through their own.

Soli Deo Gloria
Kevin M. Jones Sr.
Jarvis J. Williams
New Year's Day 2016
Louisville, Kentucky

ABBREVIATIONS

ABC	American Baptist Convention presently American Baptist Churches USA
ABHMS	American Baptist Home Mission Society
BFC	Baptist Fellowship Center
B&H	Broadman and Holman
CLC	Christian Life Commission
ERLC	Ethics & Religious Liberties Commission
ETS	Evangelical Theological Society
HBCU	Historically Black College and University
KKK	Ku Klux Klan
LXX	Septuagint
NBC	National Baptist Convention
SBC	Southern Baptist Convention
SBTS	The Southern Baptist Theological Seminary

SELECTED SOUTHERN BAPTIST CONVENTION RESOLUTIONS ON RACE FROM 1845 TO 2007[1]

1845, Augusta, Georgia: Resolution on the Colored Population— RESOLVED, That the Board of Domestic Missions be instructed to take all prudent measures, for the religious instruction of our colored population.

1849, Charleston, South Carolina: Resolution on Colored People— RESOLVED, That the pastors of our churches be affectionately requested to impart to the colored members of their charges information in relation to the African missions of the Convention, and to secure their cooperation, as far as practicable in sustaining them.

RESOLVED, That we regard the instruction of our colored population, as a duty imperatively incumbent upon us as Southern Christians; that we regard the preaching of the word of God as the best means of discharging this duty, and we earnestly recommend our churches, to devote a stated portion of

---

[1] There are at least thirty-one Southern Baptist Convention resolutions on race. For a list, see "Resolutions Search," Southern Baptist Convention, accessed July 16, 2016, http://www.sbc.net/resolutions/about/race.

their public exercises to the particular instruction of colored persons in the truths of the Bible.

1886, Montgomery, Alabama: Resolution on the Negro—RESOVLED 1st. That the work of the Home Mission Board among the colored people meets the cordial endorsement and approval of this Convention; and that said Board be authorized and empowered in their discretion to apply the sum of ten thousand dollars of the funds coming in during next year from churches and people tributary to this Convention, to the carrying on and enlarging of said work.

2nd. That our churches and congregations be earnestly requested and urged to raise the sum of ten thousand dollars for this work during next year, in addition to their ordinary contributions and as opportunity offers, to aid young colored ministers in acquiring education and more perfect training for their work.

1937, New Orleans, Louisiana: Resolution on Race—WHEREAS, We recognize the wide gulf existing between the varied practices of our modern society and the principles of Christianity;

AND WHEREAS, We feel a deep sense of shame that many of these sins and problems exist because of our indifference to them;

AND WHEREAS, We believe that a firm stand expressing our conviction and willingness to act will do much to eradicate some of these evils; therefore, be it RESOLVED.

A. International Relationships
1. We recognize that a warless world is the Christian ideal and that we Christians should throw all our weight and power into the balance for peace.

2. That we petition the President of the United States to consider the advisability of calling a conference of world powers to consider the possibility of disarmament, believing that this would do much to relieve strained international relationships which are endangering world peace at the present time.

3. That a formal letter of gratitude be sent to General and Madam Chiang Kai-Shek, expressing to them and the people of the Chinese Republic our deep appreciation for their recent gift to the flood sufferers of this country which we believe to have been a splendid expression of Christian fraternalism.

B. Labor and Agriculture
We deplore all intolerable conditions wherein economic injustice or industrial inhumanity burdens any group of our fellow human beings with poverty, with low standards of living and inequality.

C. Racial
As a body of Christians we deplore the un-Christian practices so widely prevalent in many of our racial relationships.

1939, Oklahoma City, Oklahoma: Resolution Concerning Lynching and Race Relations—1. That we record our gratitude that for the year 1938 the number of lynchings decreased and that only six lives were sacrificed to mob violence; That it brings a deep sense of sorrow and shame to us, both as citizens and Christians, that this form of lawlessness should still persist to any degree; That we pledge ourselves and urge all citizens to contend earnestly for the administration of justice under the orderly processes of law, reaffirming our unalterable opposition to all forms of mob violence.

2. That while lynching is not due wholly to racial antipathies nor the victims of lynching limited to any one race, it is beyond doubt or question that racial

antipathies are often one of the chief contributing causes; That we are glad to believe and have many good reasons to believe that as between the white and colored races within the bounds of this Convention racial animosities are growing less and racial understanding and cooperation are increasing, as indicated by the fact that the white people of the South, especially our Baptist pastors and churches, are establishing and maintaining frequent contacts of a friendly and helpful nature with the Negro race; That we urge our Baptist people everywhere to maintain and extend these friendly and helpful contacts and relations, remembering always the law of Christian obligation that the strong should bear the burdens of the weak, and yet doing this without any spirit of patronizing or air of condescending.

3. That we recognize the many inequalities and injustices which still exist in the dealings of organized society and of individuals with the Negro race and in the provision made for the advancement of the Negro race, such as the disproportionate distribution of public school funds, the lack of equal and impartial administration of justice in the courts, inadequate wages paid for Negro labor and the lack of adequate industrial and commercial opportunity for the Negro race as a whole; That we pledge ourselves as Christians and citizens to use our influence and give our efforts for the correction of these inequalities and for securing for the Negro opportunities for his full development in his education, industrial and religious life.

1941, Birmingham, Alabama: Resolution Concerning Race Relations— Be it resolved by the Southern Baptist Convention in annual session assembled:

1. That we reaffirm our deep and abiding interest in the welfare of all races of mankind, and particularly our deep and abiding interest in the welfare and advancement of the Negro race, which lives in our midst to the number of some ten or eleven million.

2. That this Convention would urge the pastors and churches affiliated with the Convention, and all our Baptist people, to cultivate and maintain the finest Christian spirit and attitude toward the Negro race, and to do everything possible for the welfare of the race, both economic and religious and for the defense and protection of all the civil rights of the race.

3. That we rejoice that the number of lynchings for 1940 was so small, being only five, but we regret that even this number of lives, two more than the year before, should have been sacrificed to mob violence, and we express our abiding determination to put forth every possible effort for the creation and maintenance of law and order and for the suppression of all mob violence throughout our land.

1944, Atlanta, Georgia: Resolution on Race—4. In view of the increasing acuteness of the race problem within the nation, and especially in the South, and the danger which crouches at our doors, that we shall be guilty of unchristian attitudes and actions, we recommend that the Convention reaffirm and lay upon the hearts of the Baptists of the South the resolutions adopted at the 1941 Convention, as follows:

"(1) That we reaffirm our deep and abiding interest in the welfare of all races of mankind, and particularly our deep and abiding interest in the welfare and advancement of the Negro race, which lives in our midst to the number of some ten or eleven millions.

(2) That this Convention would urge the pastors and churches affiliated with the Convention, and all our Baptist people, to cultivate and maintain the finest Christian spirit and attitude toward the Negro race, and to do everything possible for the welfare of the race, both economic and religious and for the defense and protection of all the civil rights of the race."

RESOLUTION ON MINISTERIAL EDUCATION FOR NEGRO BAPTISTS

In view of the appalling spiritual need for an adequately developed ministry for the vast and perilously neglected Negro host within the bounds of our Southern Baptist Convention and due to the clear indication of Providence that this is the opportune time to move forward more aggressively and on a wider scale in the help to this worthy and highly strategic cause of ministerial education for Negro Baptists, therefore be it resolved:

First, that the Convention go on record as reaffirming our loyalty and increased cooperation with the American Baptist Theological Seminary in Nashville, and

Second, that it give its vote of approval of the work of a large group of brethren of both the white and Negro races in and around New Orleans, who have in view the imperative local and regional needs projected on the basis of local self-support and with an interracial faculty and trustee organization such a school as under Divine Providence has greatly helped already in the better equipment of a considerable number of local pastors during the seven years of its existence.

Third, that the Convention thus express its approval on this local effort as a worthy missionary project as is evidenced by its rapid growth, reaching a matriculation of over two hundred students last year; also, by the fact that it has unified the seven Negro Baptist Associations numbering a constituency of over a hundred thousand Negro Baptists; and further, by its ability to attract and hold the sympathies and cooperation of the white Baptists of New Orleans who have contributed through their churches liberally for several years to its support; and further, by the approval it has received by the Baptists of the state of both races, substantially expressed through their state organization and by many prominent leaders of the National Baptist Convention and of the Southern Baptist Convention.

Finally, that we commend the Baptist Bible Institute for the large part it has taken in Negro Education through this missionary project which grew directly out of its own missionary activities and has been largely supported by a large number of its graduate student instructors who serve every year on the faculty, along with a number of Negro teachers who give their services sacrificially for a salary scarcely more than nominal.

May 11, 1944.

Signed by Volunteer Committee:

Duke K. McCall, Courts Redford
Claud B. Bowen, Chas. W. Daniel
W. H. Knight, Louie D. Newton
W. O. Carver, R. S. Jones
T. L. Holcomb, Ellis A. Fuller
E. D. Head, Thos. V. McCaul
J. Wash Watts, E. P. Alldredge

Signed by Faculty and Trustees:

C. Chas, Taylor, President of Union Seminary
Geo. W. McWaters, Dean of Union Seminary
B. Jolicoeur, Vice-President & Trustee
P. W. Raphael, Chairman Finance Committee
L. L. Scharfenstein, New Orleans
J. W. Shepard, President Emeritus
R. H. Whittington, Secretary of Board

1946, Miami, Florida: Resolution on Race—WHEREAS, This unity is now endangered by the efforts of groups that are endeavoring to breed hate and confusion in our midst, and

WHEREAS, The faith we profess and the teachings of the Lord and Master we love and serve, expressly forbid hatred one of the other, therefore be it

RESOLVED, That the Southern Baptist Convention assembled at Miami, Fla., hereby repudiates, and urges the members of the churches of the Convention to refrain from association with, all groups that exist for the purpose of fomenting strife and division within the nation on the basis of differences of race, religion and culture.

T. E. Miller, Maryland

SOCIAL SERVICE COMMISSION RECOMMENDATION
CONCERNING BAPTISTS AND RACE RELATIONS

We recommend, in the light of the relation of Southern Baptists to the racial problems of our land, and in the light of our brotherly relationship with three and a half million Negro Baptists in the South,

That the Convention appoint a committee of nine, composed of one member each from the Home Mission Board, the Commission on the American Baptist Theological Seminary, the Committee on Negro Theological Education, the Public Relations Committee and the Social Service Commission, and four additional members, to review the service now being rendered by Southern Baptists to the Negro race, to study the whole race situation, especially in its moral and religious aspects and meaning, to consider the responsibility of Baptists in the problems of adjustment of interracial relations, and make recommendations of procedure to the Convention, looking toward a larger fulfillment of our responsibility in the total situation and particularly with reference to helpful cooperation with our fellow Baptists in the Negro race.

1950, Chicago, Illinois: Social Service Committee Recommendation Concerning Race Relations (Adopted)—1. We recommend that this Convention commend the leadership of the Home Mission Board for promoting the plan of inviting Negro churches to participate in the simultaneous revival plans this year. We believe that if this plan is continued and extended next year by the local and associational planning committees and that if the Negro pastors are invited to share in the plans and promotion work of these committees, the vital cause of Christian cooperation in race relations will be greatly advanced.

2. Because the adoption of the special report on Race Relations in 1947 and the reaffirmation of the same report in 1948 put the Southern Baptist Convention on record with an outstanding statement of basic principles for the dissolution of interracial conflict and tension, we therefore recommend that our churches and individual members study seriously this "charter of faith" and these "principles of action" as a means of further solution of the race problem by providing a Christian basis of activity.

3. In view of the fact that in recent months there have been distinct and significant changes in the policies of institutions of higher learning in the secular field and in further view of the principles of action on race relations upon which we as Southern Baptists have taken a stand, we express the hope that the governing bodies of our denominational institutions, both educational and social service, will seriously explore with intelligence, conscience and compassion our Baptist responsibility in those areas of Christian service.

1961, Saint Louis, Missouri: Resolution on Race Relations—This Convention in years past has expressed itself clearly and positively on issues related to race relations. Today the solution of the race problem is a major challenge to Christian faith and action at home and abroad.

Because Southern Baptists are the largest Christian group in the area where racial tensions between whites and Negroes are most acute, we feel an especially keen sense of Christian responsibility in this hour.

We recognize that members of our churches have sincere differences of opinion as to the best course of action in this matter. On solid scriptural grounds, however, we reject mob violence as an attempted means of solving this problem. We believe that both lawless violence on one hand and unwarranted provocation on the other are outside the demands of Christ upon us all.

We believe that the race problem is a moral and spiritual as well as social problem. Southern Baptists accept the teachings of the Bible and the Commission of Christ as our sole guide of faith and practice in this area as in every other area. We cannot afford to let pride or prejudice undermine . . . either our Christian witness at home or the years of consecrated, sacrificial missionary service among all the peoples of the world.

We therefore urge all Southern Baptists to speak the truth of Christ in love as it relates to all those for whom he died. We further urge that this Convention reaffirm its conviction that every man has dignity and worth before the Lord. Let us commit ourselves as Christians to do all that we can to improve the relations among all races as a positive demonstration of the power of Christian love.

1965, Dallas, Texas: Resolution on Human Relations—WHEREAS, Southern Baptists as evangelical Christians have a major responsibility for the Christian witness both in the homeland and around the world, and

WHEREAS, The progress made toward an easing of racial tensions and a Christian solution does not match the extreme urgency reflected in current crises, and

WHEREAS, Paul in his letter to the Colossians (3:11) says "There cannot be Greek and Jew, circumcision and uncircumcision, barbarian, Scythian, bondman, freeman; but Christ is all, and in all," therefore

Be it RESOLVED, By the messengers assembled in this 108th session of the Southern Baptist Convention that we:

1. Rededicate ourselves in the spirit of Christ to a ministry of reconciliation among all men.

2. Remind ourselves that all men stand as equals at the foot of the cross without distinction for color.

3. Pledge ourselves to provide positive leadership in our communities, seeking through conciliation and understanding to obtain peaceful compliance with laws assuring equal rights for all. We further pledge ourselves to go beyond these laws in the practice of Christian love.

197. Richard W. Luebbert (Ala.) moved to amend Resolution 4 by adding the following paragraph between the second and third "Whereas."

WHEREAS, We deplore the open and premeditated violation of civil laws, the destruction of property, the shedding of human blood, or the taking of life as a means of influencing legislation or changing the social and cultural patterns.

1969, New Orleans, Louisiana: Resolution on New Orleans Hospital Integration—WHEREAS, It is the stated policy of Southern Baptist Hospital in New Orleans "to make available the services of the hospital to all people regardless of race, creed, color, national origin, or ability to pay, in such ways as to preserve human dignity and worth."

Therefore, be it RESOLVED, That this 1969 session of the Southern Baptist Convention meeting in New Orleans on June 13, 1969, request the Hospital Commission trustees to pursue this matter without delay in order to bring actual practice in line with stated policy.

RESOLUTION ON CHRISTIAN SOCIAL CONCERN

WHEREAS, The Southern Baptist Convention has consistently adopted statements on concern for a Christian posture toward people of all races, and

WHEREAS, Many Southern Baptist individuals and agencies have repeatedly expressed verbally and in concrete actions their concern for the betterment of the total well-being of all men; and

WHEREAS, Our Convention adopted "A Statement Concerning the Crisis in Our Nation" in its annual session in 1968; and

WHEREAS, The Home Mission Board has given prophetic leadership in seeking to implement the principles of "A Statement Concerning the Crisis in Our Nation"; and

WHEREAS, Many Southern Baptist laymen, pastors, and denominational leaders have consistently solicited support for governmental and social service agencies which seek to minister to the physical, material, and emotional needs of needy people of all races; and

WHEREAS, Militant leaders of some races have made widely publicized demands for racial "reparations" upon religious bodies of our nation;

Therefore, be it RESOLVED, That we as messengers to the Southern Baptist Convention in New Orleans on June 13, 1969, reaffirm our commitment to the principles embodied in the Southern Baptist Convention's "A Statement Concerning the Crisis in Our Nation" in 1968; and

Be it further RESOLVED, That we encourage the Home Mission Board and other Southern Baptist agencies to give prayerful urgency to continuing implementation of the suggestions made in "A Statement Concerning the Crisis in Our Nation"; and

Be it further RESOLVED, That we urge individuals, churches, and institutions to continue to work for the fullest possible freedom and fulfillment of aspirations for human dignity and personal worth for all people; and

Be it further RESOLVED, That we express appreciation for those persons and agencies which have made courageous efforts to work for racial justice and human betterment in difficult areas; and

Be it further RESOLVED, That we reject in total the demands, principles, and methods espoused by the National Black Economic Development Council which has made outrageous claims against religious bodies in our nation, proclaiming our disapproval of the intimidation, threats, and ultimatums propagated by leaders of this movement; and

Be it further RESOLVED, That we instruct all Southern Baptist Convention agencies to channel available funds through already established channels of Convention agencies and institutions in keeping with program assignments for interracial and social service activities; and

Be it further RESOLVED, That we call upon all citizens of whatever race, creed, or national origin to work for racial justice, economic improvement, political emancipation, educational advancement, and Christian understanding among all peoples of the nation and the world.

1970, Denver, Colorado: Resolution on Race—WHEREAS, Southern Baptists are aware of many areas of tension and misunderstanding between racial groups in our nation, and

WHEREAS, We realize that economic, social, and educational conditions make these problems more serious, and

WHEREAS, We recognize that militant extremists of whatever race do not speak or act for the vast majority of that racial group, and

WHEREAS, We reaffirm our responsibility as Christians to build bridges of good will on foundations of justice;

Therefore, be it RESOLVED, That we express gratitude to God for the progress being made in an increasing number of our churches where persons of other races are welcomed into all areas of church life and fellowship, and

Be it further RESOLVED, That we recognize with thanksgiving the growing cooperation between Baptist groups of differing races at the local, associational, state, and national levels, and

Be it further RESOLVED, That as Christians we more diligently seek to cultivate good relationships between individuals and groups who differ racially from us through joint projects for human betterment and Christian witness in church and community, and

Be it further RESOLVED, That we seek to be open to communication with those who differ from us, and work redemptively with them in the spirit of Christ for all good causes, private and public, which strengthen justice, reduce suffering, and enhance freedom.

1978, Atlanta, Georgia: Resolution on Racism—WHEREAS, Harmony between the races and justice for all persons remain a goal for American society, and

WHEREAS, The quest for racial justice and peace is a Christian concern, and

WHEREAS, The civil rights progress of the 1960's has given way to new expressions of racism in the 1970's, which exist in both individuals and the structure of society, and

WHEREAS, New racism continues to deprive minority persons of practical means of advancement, and

WHEREAS, Over 40 percent of black teenagers are unemployed in some urban areas of this nation, and

WHEREAS, According to a recent government study black persons experience discrimination three out of four times when seeking to rent housing,

Therefore, be it RESOLVED, That we seek to purge ourselves and our society of all forms of racism, and

Be it further RESOLVED, That we pledge ourselves to a renewed commitment in applying the teachings of Jesus to the practical concerns of all minority persons.

1982, New Orleans, Louisiana: Resolution on the Ku Klux Klan— WHEREAS, The Ku Klux Klan is an organization that promotes human hatred, and

WHEREAS, The Bible teaches that within the Christian family there is no racial distinction, and

WHEREAS, The gospel of Jesus Christ is to be proclaimed to all people everywhere, no matter the color of their skin.

Therefore, be it RESOLVED, That the Southern Baptist Convention in its 125th session, meeting in New Orleans, Louisiana, go on record as strongly opposing the activities of the Ku Klux Klan and specifically their most recent attempts at membership recruitment and racial terrorism.

1983, Pittsburg, Pennsylvania: Resolution on Black and Ethnic Involvement—WHEREAS, The Southern Baptist Convention now spreads from Alaska to Puerto Rico and from the Atlantic to the Pacific; and

WHEREAS, Over 5,000 churches within the Southern Baptist family represent the black and ethnic community utilizing 80 different languages; and

WHEREAS, The baptismal ratio among this segment of the family is better than 1 to 13; and

WHEREAS, Along with the numerical gains and missionary responsibility, there has been an emergence of strong leadership, pulpit ability, denominational fidelity, and administrative capability; and

WHEREAS, It is in the best interest of the Southern Baptist Convention to utilize and encourage these individuals by involving them in places of responsible leadership.

Therefore, be it RESOLVED, That we, the messengers of the Southern Baptist Convention meeting in Pittsburg, Pennsylvania, June 14-16, 1983, commend those responsible for placing ethnics and blacks on denominational programs on every denominational level; and

Be it finally RESOLVED, That we encourage all agencies, boards, and committees to seek out ethnic and black leadership from within the Southern Baptist family from all sections of our Convention to serve on boards, committees, commissions, and programs of the Southern Baptist Convention so as to reflect more completely the oneness in Christ and a stronger influence for our Lord everywhere and with everyone.

1989, Las Vegas, Nevada: Resolution on Racism—WHEREAS, Southern Baptists have not always clearly stood for racial justice and equality; and

WHEREAS, The growth in the racial and ethnic population of Southern Baptist life is a strong indicator of our growing diversity; and

WHEREAS, The Bible affirms that all people are created in the image of God and are therefore equal; and

WHEREAS, All people need a saving relationship with God through Jesus Christ;

Therefore, be it RESOLVED, That we, the messengers of the Southern Baptist Convention, meeting in Las Vegas, Nevada, June 13-15, 1989, affirm our intention of standing publicly and privately for racial justice and equality.

Be it further RESOLVED, That we repent of any past bigotry and pray for those who are still caught in its clutches; and

Be it further RESOLVED, That we bear witness to the devastating impact of racism; and

Be it further RESOLVED, That we call upon individual Southern Baptists, as well as our churches, to reach across racial boundaries, establishing fraternal rather than paternal friendships; and

Be it further RESOLVED, That we encourage Southern Baptist churches to observe Race Relations Sunday; and

Be it further RESOLVED, That our agencies and institutions seek diligently to bring about greater racial and ethnic representation at every level of Southern Baptist institutional life; and be it finally RESOLVED, That we as Southern Baptists renew our commitment to share the gospel of Jesus

Christ with every individual in obedience to the Great Commission (Matt. 28:18-20).

1993, Houston, Texas: Resolution on Racial and Ethnic Reconciliation:
WHEREAS, Southern Baptists are on record as abhorring racial and ethnic injustice; and

WHEREAS, The practice of so-called "ethnic cleansing" continues to plague the world, as demonstrated by the recent atrocities in the Balkans; and

WHEREAS, The central message of the Gospel of Jesus Christ is reconciliation to God, which should result in reconciliation to other persons regardless of racial, ethnic, social, and economic differences; and

WHEREAS, Southern Baptists are committed to taking this reconciling Gospel to all the world.

Therefore, be it RESOLVED, That we, the messengers of the Southern Baptist Convention, meeting in Houston, Texas, June 15-17, 1993, express our gratitude to God for his reconciling grace, and reaffirm our intention to love our neighbors as ourselves, denouncing in strongest terms every expression of racial and ethnic prejudice, discrimination, and hatred; and

Be it further RESOLVED, That we call upon our President and other leaders of the international community to work to end genocide wherever found; and

Be it further RESOLVED, That we call upon federal, state, and local government to enforce fully civil rights laws when such laws are in accordance with the Word of God, and to prosecute those persons who violate such laws; and

Be it finally RESOLVED, That we call upon Southern Baptists to redouble their efforts in their own communities to reach across racial and ethnical boundaries to establish both wholesome friendships and mutually beneficial ministry relationships.

1995, Atlanta, Georgia: Resolution on Racial Reconciliation on the 150th Anniversary of the Southern Baptist Convention—WHEREAS, Since its founding in 1845, the Southern Baptist Convention has been an effective instrument of God in missions, evangelism, and social ministry; and

WHEREAS, The Scriptures teach that Eve is the mother of all living (Gen 3:20), and that God shows no partiality, but in every nation whoever fears him and works righteousness is accepted by him (Acts 10:34-35), and that God has made from one blood every nation of men to dwell on the face of the earth (Acts 17:26); and

WHEREAS, Our relationship to African-Americans has been hindered from the beginning by the role that slavery played in the formation of the Southern Baptist Convention; and

WHEREAS, Many of our Southern Baptist forbears defended the right to own slaves, and either participated in, supported, or acquiesced in the particularly inhumane nature of American slavery; and

WHEREAS, In later years Southern Baptists failed, in many cases, to support, and in some cases opposed, legitimate initiatives to secure the civil rights of African-Americans; and

WHEREAS, Racism has led to discrimination, oppression, injustice, and violence, both in the Civil War and throughout the history of our nation; and

WHEREAS, Racism has divided the body of Christ and Southern Baptists in particular, and separated us from our African-American brothers and sisters; and

WHEREAS, Many of our congregations have intentionally and/or unintentionally excluded African-Americans from worship, membership, and leadership; and

WHEREAS, Racism profoundly distorts our understanding of Christian morality, leading some Southern Baptists to believe that racial prejudice and discrimination are compatible with the Gospel; and

WHEREAS, Jesus performed the ministry of reconciliation to restore sinners to a right relationship with the Heavenly Father, and to establish right relations among all human beings, especially within the family of faith.

Therefore, be it RESOLVED, That we, the messengers to the Sesquicentennial meeting of the Southern Baptist Convention, assembled in Atlanta, Georgia, June 20-22, 1995, unwaveringly denounce racism, in all its forms, as deplorable sin; and

Be it further RESOLVED, That we affirm the Bible's teaching that every human life is sacred, and is of equal and immeasurable worth, made in God's image, regardless of race or ethnicity (Gen 1:27), and that, with respect to salvation through Christ, there is neither Jew nor Greek, there is neither slave nor free, there is neither male nor female, for (we) are all one in Christ Jesus (Gal 3:28); and

Be it further RESOLVED, That we lament and repudiate historic acts of evil such as slavery from which we continue to reap a bitter harvest, and we recognize that the racism which yet plagues our culture today is inextricably tied to the past; and

Be it further RESOLVED, That we apologize to all African-Americans for condoning and/or perpetuating individual and systemic racism in our lifetime; and we genuinely repent of racism of which we have been guilty, whether consciously (Psalm 19:13) or unconsciously (Leviticus 4:27); and

Be it further RESOLVED, That we ask forgiveness from our African-American brothers and sisters, acknowledging that our own healing is at stake; and

Be it further RESOLVED, That we hereby commit ourselves to eradicate racism in all its forms from Southern Baptist life and ministry; and

Be it further RESOLVED, That we commit ourselves to be doers of the Word (James 1:22) by pursuing racial reconciliation in all our relationships, especially with our brothers and sisters in Christ (1 John 2:6), to the end that our light would so shine before others, that they may see (our) good works and glorify (our) Father in heaven (Matthew 5:16); and

Be it finally RESOLVED, That we pledge our commitment to the Great Commission task of making disciples of all people (Matt 28:19), confessing that in the church God is calling together one people from every tribe and nation (Rev 5:9), and proclaiming that the Gospel of our Lord Jesus Christ is the only certain and sufficient ground upon which redeemed persons will stand together in restored family union as joint-heirs with Christ (Rom 8:17).

1996, New Orleans, Louisiana: Resolution on the Arson of African-American Churches—WHEREAS, In the past 18 months there have been at least 30 arson-blamed [fires] at African-American churches; and

WHEREAS, The desecration and destruction of churches is a particularly heinous form of hatred; and

WHEREAS, Violence against churches risks crippling one of society's most effective institutions for mediation and reconciliation; and

WHEREAS, Racial bigotry in all its forms is absolutely contrary to the tenets of biblical Christianity; and

WHEREAS, Attacks against any church constitute an attack against the entire believing community; and

WHEREAS, Christians are enjoined to bear one another's burdens (Galatians 6:2); and

WHEREAS, The Southern Baptist Convention is on record for its vigorous opposition to racial injustice and is taking significant steps toward racial reconciliation; Now, therefore,

BE IT RESOLVED, That we the messengers of the Southern Baptist Convention meeting June 11-13, 1996, in New Orleans, Louisiana, do hereby deplore these despicable and abominable acts of lawlessness and racism; and

BE IT FURTHER RESOLVED, That we pledge to pray for, support, encourage, stand with, and assist our sister churches and fellow believers in the African-American community who have been victims of these criminal acts; and

BE IT FURTHER RESOLVED, That we target our efforts toward racial reconciliation in those communities hardest hit by racial violence against churches; and

FINALLY, BE IT THEREFORE RESOLVED, That we call upon local, state, and federal governments to investigate promptly and vigorously these hate crimes, apprehend those who are responsible for these cowardly acts of bigotry, and prosecute perpetrators of church arson to the fullest extent of the law.

2007, San Antonio, Texas: On the 150th Anniversary of the Dred Scott Decision—WHEREAS, March 6, 2007, marked the 150th anniversary of the infamous Dred Scott Decision by the United States Supreme Court; and

WHEREAS, The majority opinion of the Court concluded that people of African ancestry and their descendants "had no rights which the white man was bound to respect" and ruled that an entire race of people did not have personhood nor right of citizenship; and

WHEREAS, We affirm the Declaration of Independence which says, "we hold these truths to be self-evident that all men are created equal and are endowed by their Creator with certain inalienable rights"; and

WHEREAS, This deplorable decision required action by all three branches of government to eventually overturn: Emancipation Proclamation (1863); Brown v. Board of Education (1954); and Civil Rights Act of 1964; and

WHEREAS, We are complicit with this erroneous Supreme Court decision when we fail to love, minister to, and share the Gospel with people because of their ethnicity, ability, or station in life; and

WHEREAS, We are all born as slaves to sin and have no rights to the throne of God except through Jesus Christ; now, therefore, be it

RESOLVED, That the messengers to the Southern Baptist Convention meeting in San Antonio, Texas, June 12-13, 2007, wholly lament and repudiate the Dred Scott Decision and fully embrace the Lord's command to love our neighbors as ourselves; and be it further

RESOLVED, That we reaffirm the historic action in 1995 of the Southern Baptist Convention to "unwaveringly denounce racism, in all its forms, as deplorable sin," and to view "every human life as sacred . . . of equal and immeasurable worth, made in God's image, regardless of race or ethnicity"; and be it further

RESOLVED, That we fully concur that "racism profoundly distorts our understanding of Christian morality"; and be it further

RESOLVED, That we commend our churches who intentionally reach out to all persons regardless of ethnicity, and we encourage all other Southern Baptist churches to emulate their example, as the Body of Christ is commanded and called to do; and be it finally

RESOLVED, That we pray for and eagerly await the day that the scourge and blight of racism is totally eradicated from the Body of Christ so that the world may see the love of Christ incarnated in and through us.

CHAPTER 1

Conceived in Sin, Called by the Gospel: The Root Cause of the Stain of Racism in the Southern Baptist Convention

R. Albert Mohler Jr.

Behold, I was brought forth in iniquity, and in sin did my mother conceive me" (Ps 51:5 ESV). This crucial verse from the Psalter of Israel rings in the memory of most Christians. David is pouring out his heart after Nathan the prophet confronts the king with his sin, a sin that meant the death of another man and the taking of that other man's wife. David, filled with remorse and repentant of his sin, traces that sin back to the moment of his conception. Where else can he trace it? His sin is his own from the beginning of his existence.

Rightly understood, the human story is David's story. From the moment Adam and Eve disobeyed God, sin has distorted and corrupted human existence and every dimension of human life. Since Eden, anything humanity touches is marked by our sin. Perhaps one of the saddest and most sordid evidences of the fall and its horrifying effects is the ideology of racism. Throughout history racial ideologies have been driving forces of war, of social cohesion, of demagoguery, and of dictatorships. Race theory was central to the Nazi regime and was used by both sides in the Pacific theater of World War II. In that theater of the war, both the Japanese and the Americans claimed the other was an inferior race that must be defeated by force. The Japanese claimed racial superiority as central to their subjugation of other Asian peoples.

At the same time many white Americans claimed and assumed the superiority of white skin to black and brown skin or to any other color of skin. The main "color line," as Frederick Douglass called it in 1881, has always been black and white in America. While this is a national problem and theories of racial superiority have been popular in both the North and the South, the states of the old Confederacy gave those ideologies their most fertile soil. White superiority was claimed as a belief by both Abraham Lincoln and Jefferson Davis, but the Confederacy made racial superiority a central purpose. More humbling still is the fact that many churches, churchmen, and theologians gave sanction to that ideology of racial superiority. While this was true throughout the southern churches, Southern Baptists bear a particular responsibility and burden of history.

Historians date the founding of the Southern Baptist Convention to 1845, when representatives from Baptist churches in the South gathered to create a new Baptist missionary-sending organization. They gathered because the existing national convention's missionary-sending societies had decided not to send missionary candidates who were slaveholders. William B. Johnson, the first president of the SBC, acknowledged what he called "the peculiar circumstances in which the organization of the Southern Baptist Convention became necessary." Those particular circumstances had everything to do with slavery. Baptists in the South were outraged that they were being asked to give financial support to mission societies that would no longer send slaveholding candidates to the mission fields.

They were also outraged that slavery was the dividing line. After all, they argued, Baptists in the North had only fairly recently decided that slavery was evil, and their own cities and states had benefitted richly from northern dominance in the slave trade for generations. Methodists in the North and the South had already divided over the issue. After the Baptist split, Presbyterians likewise divided. The issue was the same. The issue was slavery. Indeed, we cannot tell the story of the Southern Baptist Convention without starting with slavery. In fact, the SBC was not only founded by slaveholders; it was founded by men who held to an ideology of racial superiority and who bathed that ideology in scandalous theological argument. At times white superiority was defended by a putrid exegesis of the Bible that claimed a "curse of Ham" as the explanation of dark skin, an argument that reflects such ignorance of Scripture and such shameful exegesis that it could only be believed by those who were looking for an argument to satisfy their prejudices.

The founders of the SBC would insist that the ultimate issue was the Great Commission. Missions, faithfulness to the Great Commission, was indeed the cause of the convention. But history proves slavery was the cause of its founding. Further, notable Southern Baptists James P. Boyce and John Broadus, founders of The Southern Baptist Theological Seminary, were chaplains in the Confederate Army. Just a few months ago I was reading a history of Greenville, South Carolina, when I came across a racist statement made by James P. Boyce, my ultimate predecessor as president of SBTS. It was so striking that I had to find a chair. This is a staggering moral fact, and it raises many urgent questions. How can a missionary convention conceived in race-based slavery become or remain a viable and honorable force for the gospel of Jesus Christ? Put in the larger historical context, the questions grow even more vexing. How could the nation itself, supposedly "conceived in liberty," have been simultaneously conceived in racism?

Even most abolitionists were racists. Racial segregation was legal in the United States for most of the twentieth century. Racism is so insidious that it appears even where it is declared to have been eradicated. In 1995, on the

150th anniversary of the founding of the SBC, the denomination publicly repudiated its roots in the defense of slavery. That was a start, a horribly delayed but important start. Today far more is required of us. Repudiating slavery is not enough. We must repent and seek to confront and remove every strain of racism that remains and seek with all our strength to be the kind of churches of which Jesus would be proud, the kind of churches that will look like the marriage supper of the Lamb.

The separation of humans into ranks of superiority and inferiority differentiated by skin color is a direct assault on the doctrine of creation and an insult to the *imago Dei*, the image of God in which every human is made. Racial superiority is also directly subversive of the gospel of Christ, effectively denying the full power of his substitutionary atonement and undermining the faithful preaching of the gospel to all persons and to all nations. We still see racism in both covert and stunning overt forms. Every society shows the stain in every epoch. Every human heart reveals the stain. This brings us back to Psalm 51:5, which reminds us that even Israel's greatest king, one described in Scripture as "a man after [God's] own heart" (Acts 13:22 NIV), was "brought forth in iniquity" (ESV) and conceived in sin. And yet the Messiah sits enthroned upon King David's throne.

How can good and even greatness come out of such evil? Can a man conceived in sin, even an adulterer and a murderer, become useful to God? If so, what about the racist? Is even a racist able to become saved and transformed by the power of the gospel? The gospel offers an emphatic yes! Both individual racists and even an entire convention of churches conceived in sin can in fact be transformed by the gospel.

One key to our understanding must be David's heartfelt cry: "Have mercy on me, O God, according to your steadfast love; according to your abundant mercy blot out my transgressions. Wash me thoroughly from my iniquity, and cleanse me from my sin!" (Ps 51:1–2 ESV). That has to be the starting point for the SBC as well. Our confidence is not in our ability to extricate ourselves from the stain of racism. We have no such power. But God does, according to his steadfast love and his abundant mercy.

A new generation of Southern Baptists bears the responsibility to beg God for his abundant mercy and steadfast love in transforming this convention of missionary churches and its people, removing racism stain by stain as a sign to the world of the power of the gospel of Christ. We cannot change the past, but we must learn from it. We have no way to confront the dead with their heresies, but neither do we have any way to avoid the reckoning we must make and the repentance that must be our own. The legacy of the SBC and its present influence and reach are great. But our commitment to Christ requires that we confess in every generation the sin in which this convention was conceived and the sin that remains, while working relentlessly to see racists within our convention redeemed from the powerful effects of this sin.

As we look across the cultural landscape, we see racial injustice and systemic wrong. We also recognize that the church, including the SBC, has often been on the wrong side of these issues. This is why the gospel needs to be preached to the church even before the church preaches the gospel to the world. We are the stewards of the only story that saves, the only story that leads to the healing of the nations and the gathering of a new humanity in Christ. The gospel is the only story that offers real hope and celebrates what the world fears. Principalities and powers offer many plans but no real hope. The gospel offers a hope that celebrates the breaking down of ethnic barriers and celebrates the sound of the gospel in different languages and tongues.

We must look forward to that day when the table of the Lord will be set and all the nations will live in light of the Father and of the Lamb. Diversity is not an accident or a problem; it is a sign of God's providence and promise. If the church gets this wrong, it is not just getting race and ethnic difference wrong. It is getting the gospel wrong. We cannot obey the Great Commission without celebrating the glory of the new humanity only Christ can create. For now we must humble ourselves and confront our responsibility—our own responsibility—to oppose the stain of racism with the resolve of a peo-ple saved only by grace.

"In sin did my mother conceive me" (Ps 51:5 ESV). How can anything good or righteous or true to the gospel follow those words? The answer is only by the power of Almighty God. By God's grace alone, being conceived in sin is not the end of the story. The SBC is a fellowship of churches deter-mined to follow Christ's call to the nations and to our nation. The SBC was conceived in sin and is called by the gospel. The stain of racism is real—all too real—but the power of the gospel is grace greater than all our sin!

CHAPTER 2

Historical Causes of the Stain of Racism in the Southern Baptist Convention

MATTHEW J. HALL

Southern Baptists are more haunted by the ghosts of white supremacy and racism than most denominations. While the specter of racialized injustice and evil left no corner of American religious life untouched, our family of churches has had a particularly sordid and tragic part to play in this story. In fact, we helped invent the ghosts themselves and then baptized them in pseudo biblical and theological categories.

Reconciliation is the goal. We certainly want to remove the stain of racism from our Southern Baptist Convention. But we want more than that. We want to see an SBC that is made up of churches that represent the diversity of the kingdom of God. In our fellowship—our *koinonia*—we bear testimony for good or for ill. We want to see the power of the gospel at work, tearing down the dividing wall of race.

That kind of demolition—a critical part of reconciliation—requires some difficult elements. To begin, it requires telling the truth, especially about our past. We know this to be true in our individual relationships.

We understand full well that two persons cannot be truly reconciled to each other without a clear acknowledgment of wrongdoing, confession of it, and the exchange of forgiveness. This is, at its core, a profoundly Christian vision.

We seem to struggle to understand what reconciliation would require of groups of persons, including groups of Christians. But for us, as a convention of churches, to see true gospel reconciliation within our fellowship, a measure of historical truth-telling is required—a stance that is not always comfortable, popular, or simple. Instead, talking about it will be difficult; it will provoke those who refuse to acknowledge the past, and it will remind us that these are complex issues.

White Baptists and the Hypocrisy of Freedom

Long before the founding of the Southern Baptist Convention in 1845, white Baptists in the South were laying the foundation for a society built on racial hierarchy. The irony is that as they did, they were also the leading voices calling for religious liberty. These bold voices were often among those most complicit in a system that treated black bodies as commodities to be bought and sold. For example, John "Swearing Jack" Waller was an early Virginia Baptist imprisoned for not obtaining a preaching license. However, he was also a slaveholder who seemed not to find any contradiction in advocating for liberty and owning other humans.[1]

John Leland, one of the most prominent advocates of religious liberty, provides another complicated example. At one time Leland advocated for an abolitionist position. But as he grew older, the Virginia Baptist landed on an ardent pro-slavery position. By the time he relocated to New England, he had begun to argue that slavery was a civil or political issue, not a religious

---

[1] Bill J. Leonard, *Baptists in America* (New York: Columbia University Press, 2005), 161.

one.[2] Leland's argument was common in its day and endured throughout southern religion. For two centuries, those that defended the racialized status quo routinely used one form or another of this argument to silence the church's witness on slavery, segregation, lynching, rape, and racial injustice.

Of course, what was true of these white Baptists was true more generally of this generation of white Americans. Those figures we are most prone to admire—including leading men such as Jonathan Edwards and George Whitefield—seemed entirely blind to the wickedness of American slavery. How could those most courageous for the sake of independence and liberty also be among those most enriched by the slave system? Our national story is complex, as is our denominational story.

The Birth of the Southern Baptist Convention and Racism

Our own denomination was birthed out of a commitment to preserve and defend slavery. We cannot evade that historical fact.[3] Along with Presbyterians and Methodists, Baptists broke their national fellowship over the morality of slave ownership. The nomination of James Reeve, a Georgia Baptist and slaveholder, to serve as a missionary through the American Baptist Home Mission Society (ABHMS) was a clear test intended to force the society's hand one way or another, to take sides with either abolitionists or with slavery's defenders. The ABHMS chose not to receive the application, thereby trying to avoid making any pronouncement on the issue. When Alabama Baptists subsequently wrote to the Triennial Convention, headquartered in Boston, regarding the board's disposition toward appointing slaveholders to foreign mission work, things took a more concrete form. The board members

---

[2] Bruce Gourley, "John Leland: Evolving Views of Slavery, 1789–1839," *Baptist History and Heritage Journal* (40:1 Winter 2005), 104–16.

[3] For more on this, see C. C. Goen, *Broken Churches, Broken Nation* (Macon: Mercer University Press, 1997). Thomas S. Kidd and Barry Hankins, *Baptists in America: History* (New York: Oxford University Press, 2015).

replied: "If . . . any one should offer himself as a missionary, having slaves, and should insist on retaining them as his property, we could not appoint them. One thing is certain, we can never be a party to any arrangement which would imply approbation of slavery."[4] In response, by May 1845 white delegates from the deep South gathered in Augusta, Georgia, and formed a new mission society, the Southern Baptist Convention. The majority of the 293 delegates came from Georgia and South Carolina. After organizing the new fellowship, forged in defense of slavery, the distinguished guests ironically joined together to sing "Blest Be the Tie That Binds."

The formation of the Southern Baptist Convention in 1845 preceded Southern states' secession from the Union by fifteen years. By the time secession arrived in 1860, Southern Baptist support for the South's "peculiar institution" had further hardened. Not all supported secession. But virtually all supported slavery. James P. Boyce provides one example. Boyce, scion of a prominent South Carolina planter family, plainly articulated his discomfort with secession. However, his opposition to the Confederate break was due to a fear that war would result in the demise of slavery. He declared himself to be "an ultra-slavery man."[5]

Among Southern Baptist leaders, the cause of the Civil War was clear. "Slavery is the only issue," argued Samuel Boykin, editor of the *Christian Index*. "The United States is fighting against the Confederate States for slavery." At The Southern Baptist Theological Seminary, all four founding faculty were slaveholders. These men typified the "gentlemen theologians" of the South, deeply tied to the planter class and invested in the slave system. In turn they were willing to identify slavery as the beneficial means by which God had providentially introduced the Christian gospel to millions of otherwise unevangelized Africans. For example, Basil Manly Jr. concluded that "their introduction into this country has been, in the providence of God,

---

[4] Quoted in Goen, *Broken Churches, Broken Nation*, 95.
[5] Quoted in Kidd and Hankins, *Baptists in America*, 135.

instrumental in saving more of their race from heathenism, than the united membership of all the churches which foreign missions have planted."[6] This kind of rationale took a legitimate biblical principle—the providential rule of God over all the affairs of his creation—and then used it to smooth out the hard edges of the wickedness of kidnapping and selling Africans.

After the Civil War and emancipation, Southern Baptists had to try to put life back together. Of course, they could not. Life would never be the same, mercifully. But white southerners' racialized worldview only hardened, and Southern Baptists were not exempt. Basil Manly Jr. wrote to his brother in 1868, affirming, "I should be satisfied—to live and raise my child in a 'white man's country'—and if I get a chance to do so, I may accept it."[7] Southern Baptists increasingly became among the leading voices for a segregated South, calling for the preservation of white supremacy. This voice could even be heard from denominational agencies when they spoke of the status of freed black men and women. For example, the Home Mission Board declared, "Nothing is plainer to anyone who knows this race than its perfect willingness to accept a subordinate place."[8]

For their part black Baptists quickly developed their own formalized networks of churches. While the SBC included roughly 650,000 churches before the war, their numbers declined significantly after the conflict when emancipated slaves rushed out of their former churches to begin their own new churches and associations.[9] For example, in Kentucky messengers from a network of twelve black churches gathered in August 1865 to establish the State Convention of Colored Baptists. Over the years courageous leaders built

---

[6] Gregory Wills, *The Southern Baptist Theological Seminary, 1859–2009* (New York: Oxford University Press, 2009), 57–58.

[7] Quoted in Paul Harvey, *Redeeming the South: Religious Cultures and Racial Identities Among Southern Baptists, 1865–1925* (Chapel Hill: University of North Carolina Press, 1997), 32.

[8] Quoted in ibid., 40.

[9] Ibid., 22.

it into a powerful group of churches, now named the General Association of Baptists in Kentucky. In most cases black Baptists knew they were not welcome in fellowship with white Baptists.[10]

Southern Baptists, Jim Crow, and Civil Rights

The ascent of Jim Crowism—a pervasive system of legalized racial hierarchy—profoundly shaped the South. While northern cities and states often had their own de facto segregation and injustice, southern states were built on a legal code that perpetuated the mythology of "separate but equal." Biological scientific racism had been infused into old attitudes, paired with constant anxieties about interracial marriage and sexual contact. For many white southerners, including Southern Baptists, the danger of blurring the lines of segregation was tied to fears of miscegenation.

As the black freedom movement gained momentum in the decades after World War II, white southerners hardened their resolve to resist change. The Ku Klux Klan remained, but for many white southerners, including those that filled many Baptist pews, White Citizens Councils provided a more middle-class and presumably respectable form of resistance.[11] And Southern Baptists were right in the middle of it all. In fact, they were often leading the charge.

As a white Southern Baptist and a historian, I feel profound emotional disturbance that people just like me wrote some of the most dehumanizing things imaginable about other men and women created in the image of God. While many Southern Baptists would not resort to some of these most strident forms of racist attack, they found more supposedly respectable ways to delegitimize the Civil Rights Movement. Among the most common was

---

[10] Luke E. Harlow, *Religion, Race, and the Making of Confederate Kentucky, 1830–1880* (New York: Cambridge University Press, 2014), 213.

[11] For more on this, see Carolyn R. DuPont, *Mississippi Praying: Southern White Evangelicals and the Civil Rights Movement, 1945–1975* (New York: New York University Press, 2013).

to argue that civil rights leaders were Communists intent on undermining American democracy and on fomenting sexual chaos through racial inter-marriage. I have read letters from well-known figures, from local associations, and from countless congregations attacking the Civil Rights Movement, its leaders, and anyone who would lend support to the cause. These white Baptists trafficked in the myth of a friendly and peaceful South that had only been disrupted by "outside agitators." They had never actually noticed that their black brothers and sisters might as well have lived in an entirely dif-ferent world in the South. Those white Baptists were pastors, deacons, and laypeople just like me. And that scares me to death.

Historian Edward Baptist has claimed, "Whenever we dredge up the past, we find that the rusty old chains we rake from the bottom are connected to some people's present-day pains and others' contemporary privilege."[12] I think Baptist has it exactly right. Getting the story right is often painful. It exposes why some people have suffered for so long, and it also shows how others have experienced privileges of which they may not even be aware. But something in this is profoundly Christian. One reason I need to know this story, learn this story, and tell this story is for myself. I need to be reminded of the depravity of the human heart. Southern Baptists much like me were seduced by the lies and fears of Jim Crowism and racial hierarchy. Most of them did not wear white hoods and burn crosses. In fact, they would have looked down on those who did. But they carried the same hidden wounds within their souls. Telling the truth about our denomination's past is thus a powerful and constant inoculating force, reminding me that I must test all things by the Scriptures, that I must listen well to my brothers and sisters in Christ—especially those who are the least like me in the eyes of the world—and that I desperately need the humbling grace of the Spirit.

---

[12] Edward E. Baptist, "Teaching Slavery to Reluctant Listeners," *New York Times Sunday Magazine*, September 11, 2015, accessed July 16, 2016, http://www.nytimes .com/2015/09/13/magazine/teaching-slavery-to-reluctant-listeners.html?_r=0.

The symbols and artifacts of racial injustice are all around us in the Southern Baptist Convention. They are the names of buildings many of us walk in and out of every day. They are tied to the fortunes that propped up many of our institutions. We do ourselves no favors by trying to rewrite or whitewash the past, telling romanticized lies about a so-called "lost cause" and half-truths about the nature of our denominational origins. But I am not sure we foster reconciliation by attempting to efface all those symbols and artifacts either. Sure, we could rename the buildings named after white supremacists. Maybe we should. We could do away with the names of slave-holders on endowments and statues. And perhaps we should with many of them. Certainly white Southern Baptists need to listen to our black and brown brothers and sisters before settling that too hastily. But I am also convinced that we need to make sure we allow the ghosts of our racist forebears to haunt us. We need to be reminded often that we are no different from them and that we are just as susceptible to hatred, pride, and wickedness apart from the mercy and grace of God. Those ghosts can serve us well, even if painfully, by reminding us of the truth and by calling us anew to repentance and a commitment to intentionally pursue an SBC that reflects the beauty of the diversity of the kingdom of God.

CHAPTER 3

Biblical Steps Toward Removing the Stain of Racism from the Southern Baptist Convention

JARVIS J. WILLIAMS

As an African-American, multiracial, Southern Baptist, evangelical, New Testament scholar, I live in a complicated, diverse, and divided world.[1] As a faculty member of The Southern Baptist Theological Seminary, I teach in a predominately white evangelical, Southern Baptist context where most of my colleagues and students are white. As an evangelical, Southern Baptist preacher, I preach and teach often in predominately white evangelical contexts in the Southern Baptist Convention and in some predominately black, brown, and multiethnic contexts in the broader evangelical movement. As a member of and a contributor to the academic guild of New Testament scholarship, I spend most of my time critically engaging black, brown, white, multiracial, and various international scholars from different parts of the globe in

---

[1] Portions of this chapter have been published in Jarvis J. Williams, *One New Man: The Cross and Racial Reconciliation in Pauline Theology* (Nashville: B&H, 2010). Material has been published here with permission.

15

my academic publications and at various professional academic societies. At times these interactions extend beyond an evangelical and even a Christian context. These are vastly different venues, but each one plays a vital role in shaping me as an African-American, multiracial, evangelical, and Southern Baptist scholar and churchman of color with a diverse ethnic heritage.

However, I am often shocked by the degree to which I disagree with both white Southern Baptists and with black and brown Christians in general on matters of race, although we have many things in common theologically. I've observed that at times certain white Christians have difficulty talking about race or admitting that talking about race and racism is an important and necessary step toward gospel reconciliation. Some white Christians wonder whether talking about race issues is helpful at all since these discussions often reinforce racial tensions among blacks, whites, and other races in the US.

If you think only white Christians are guilty of this error, think again. In twenty years of pursuing gospel racial reconciliation in the church, I've discovered that certain black and brown evangelicals in general and certain black and brown Southern Baptists in particular, whose lives are assimilated within a predominately white Christian context, also at times wonder whether talking about race is helpful in promoting gospel unity. They too may angrily recoil against racial discussions, just as certain white Christians do. Their reactions perhaps come from fear that talking about race as black and brown Christians within a white majority evangelical context may cause them to lose some of the social privileges they have obtained from the white majority (e.g., jobs, invitations to certain conferences).

In this chapter I hope to do the following. First, I offer some personal and historical reasons ongoing racial discussions are necessary to remove the stain of racism from the SBC. Second, I offer a few biblical reasons Southern Baptists from every racial stripe should continue to work toward removing the stain of racism from their churches, from their homes, and from every aspect of SBC life. Third, I offer fifteen exhortations to Southern

Baptists on fostering multiethnic gospel partnerships in their churches and communities.

My Story

I grew up in a small and racist town in eastern Kentucky. My father was African-American. My mother's side of the family has African-American, Anglo, and Cherokee Indian blood flowing through their veins. Growing up, I heard both blacks and whites call me all sorts of racist slurs. Some whites called me nigger because I am African-American. Some blacks called me half-breed, high yellow, nigger-white, red bone, and Uncle Tom because of my multiethnic heritage and because some of them did not think that I was black enough—I still do not know what "black enough" means or who determines whether one is "black enough."

I was almost always the only black person on my athletic teams through-out my childhood and teenage years. With the exception of my uncle, all of my athletic coaches were white, most of my teammates were white, and many of them had little, if any, social interaction with black people apart from sports or the images they saw on television. I played sports for at least two racist coaches. One coach called me a racist slur to my face after a game. Another allegedly played less talented white players in front of me because I was black. All of my teachers were white with the exception of a black substitute in elementary school.

During my freshman year of high school in the early 1990s, a gang of white students attacked one of our school's few black students, and a white teacher slammed the black student against the lockers to break up the fight, although the gang of white students had assaulted him. To the surprise of the few black students and their families, the white principal put both the black student and the white students, who started the fight, in detention together. But the black student was the victim, not the perpetrator. When word spread that some of these same white students planned to attack me because they did not like blacks and because, ironically, they thought I was not black enough—do you see the arrogance and the irony of racism?—the best that one of my white teachers could say to me was "watch your back."

While I was in high school, my uncle had to explain to me why I, a black kid, needed to be careful when taking a white girl to the local drive-in theater—and this was in 1996! I also had at least a couple of racist high school teachers. One teacher had a practice of saying nigger in a class of mostly white students. During the Christmas season, in another predominately white class, one of my teachers jokingly asked me something along the lines of "Jarvis, is there a black Santa Claus for black people?"

When my high school basketball team traveled to certain racist communities to play games, one of my family members would always take appropriate measures within the law to protect me and him just in case white supremacists in the community planned a racially motivated crime against him or me during the game. During a high school basketball game, someone from the opposing team shouted at me, "Shoot it, nigger." And at a baseball game, after I struck out, someone exclaimed, "We struck out that nigger."

When I was seventeen, in 1996, the Lord Jesus saved me by means of a tragedy. My dear friend Merri Kathryn Prater (a white Southern Baptist, also seventeen) died after a car accident from a severe brain injury. Her mother Ella Prater was my senior English teacher. She too was a Southern Baptist. The Lord used Merri's death, Mrs. Prater, her husband Willie, Pastor Michael Caudill, and the Hindman First Baptist Church to lead me to faith in Christ and nourish me in that faith. My little eastern Kentucky town had no "black" churches because the town had few black people and even fewer black Christians. But this small and predominately white Southern Baptist church became my spiritual family, and God used it mightily to transform my life. In fact, this church loved me and cared for me more than distant relatives who scoffed at my conversion and chastised me for joining "a white church."

When I joined First Baptist in 1996, I became the first African-American member in the church's history. A year later my uncle became the second, and he remains the only African-American member. This congregation personified racial reconciliation. Perhaps a minority within the congregation had some reservations about a black kid (who at the time had a white girlfriend) joining their church. I can honestly say I heard no whisperings of this from anyone in the congregation. But the pastor strongly rebuked from the pulpit those from the community who stated that they would not attend the church because black people were members. Such racism shocked me because of its impact on the church. Since then I've discovered the denomination I love and of which I'm a member came into existence in part because of white supremacy and violent racism. I've additionally learned that the evangelical movement in this country was also born within an environment of racial injustice toward black people.[2]

While working on my first master's degree, I took two church history courses. But I heard few lectures about the positive role of Africans, African-Americans, or other non-Anglo Christians in the Christian movement. I took a Baptist history course. But I neither heard any lectures on nor was I required to read books about the contributions of African-American Baptists or Latin American Baptists to the Baptist movement. I took a class on English Puritanism. But I neither heard any lectures about nor was I required to read books on the Puritans' interactions with black people. Today many Southern Baptists reveal that the stain of racism remains in the SBC by their insensitive responses to incontrovertible examples of racial injustice in the US.

In my view, however, among the most significant instances of racial disparity in Southern Baptist life is intellectual racism. Intellectual racism is

---

[2] For a detailed sociological analysis that argues this point, see Michael Emerson and Christian Smith, *Divided by Faith: Evangelical Religion and the Problem of Race in America* (New York: Oxford University Press, 2001).

present in both Baptist schools and churches. Black and brown scholarship is either dismissed or ignored in many colleges, universities, and seminaries. Most Baptist colleges, universities, and seminaries have an overwhelming number of white leaders but few, if any, black and brown leaders. Few Southern Baptist churches have multiethnic or minority leaders.

Intellectual racism can also be seen in mainline white evangelical presses. Most books published by mainline presses are written by white men. Most of the books and curricula published by SBC entities are written by whites for middle-class white contexts. Few curricula address issues unique to black and brown Southern Baptist communities (e.g., systemic racism, mass incarceration, the challenges of being a Christian in an urban context).

In many cases black and brown intellectuals are not taken seriously by evangelicals in general or by Southern Baptists in particular unless some prominent white evangelical imprints his stamp of approval on them. Certain leaders and church members within the SBC still view black or brown people as intellectually or theologically suspect until they prove themselves otherwise. Therefore, as an African-American evangelical and Southern Baptist scholar and churchman with a multiracial background, and as a man who deeply loves the SBC and who has received so much good from Southern Baptists, erasing the stain of racism from our denomination deeply matters to me.

I want to add a word about this before I offer some biblical and practical steps to help Southern Baptists remove the stain of racism from our convention and from the sixteen million Southern Baptists and the 46,125 churches they represent.

White Supremacy and the Construct of Race

Theologically, the stain of racism exists in the SBC because of sin. Adam's transgression damaged both humanity's vertical (Genesis 1–3) and horizontal (Genesis 4) relationships. Historically, the stain of racism exists in the

SBC because of the enduring effects of white-supremacist thinking. White supremacy had its racist fangs in the ideology of American culture from this country's beginning and from the founding of the SBC in 1845.

Thomas Jefferson, one of America's founding fathers, believed blacks were naturally inferior to whites. In his *Notes on the State of Virginia*, Jefferson stated, "I advance it therefore as a suspicion only, that the blacks, whether originally a distinct race, or made distinct by time and circumstances, are inferior to the whites in the endowments both of body and mind" (Jefferson, *Notes on the State of Virginia*, 138–43). To be fair, Jefferson's notes state only that this was his "suspicion." Yet Jefferson is the same man who signed the Declaration of Independence, which affirmed "all men are created equal."

Jefferson, along with many other founding fathers, embraced the white supremacist idea that the white race was superior to the black race. Similarly, the first president of the SBC, William Bullein Johnson (1845–1851), believed in black inferiority. He was a pro-slavery president of a pro-slavery SBC. But from where did the American construct of race and white supremacy come? Why does white supremacy still exist? And why do many Southern Baptists continue to embrace this racist construct?

The English term *race* first referenced human beings as a term of classification in the sixteenth century. In the eighteenth century, the term *race* was broadly applied to the diverse populations of Native Americans, Africans, and Europeans in England's American colonies. In this historical context the term *race* developed to reference a hierarchal ranking system, which reflected English attitudes toward diverse groups of people. Conquered Indians were segregated from Europeans and exploited or expelled from their lands. The enslavement of Africans and their offspring was institutionalized in the late seventeenth and early eighteenth centuries. By then many Africans were identified as property.[3]

---

[3] Audrey Smedley, "Race," in *Oxford Companion to United States History* (Oxford: Oxford University Press, 2001), 641–45, esp. 641.

In the eighteenth century European scientists collected data and arranged materials about newly discovered people in the New World, Asia, and Africa. Scientists like Carl Linnaeus (1707–1778) and Johann Blumenbach (1752–1850) thought different groups represented variants within a human species. As a result, they constructed "racial" categories based on skin color and other physical characteristics. Their method often incorporated anecdotal data from travelers, missionaries, merchants, and sailors instead of depending on scientific observation alone. Eventually, these descriptions and classifications of diverse people entered the learned communities in Europe and America, where they were appropriated to support folk ideas about human differences.[4]

Eighteenth-century antislavery sentiments threatened the system of American slavery. In response, advocates of slavery developed new and stronger rationalizations for the institution by focusing on the slaves' nature and by hyperbolically explaining the differences between Africans and Europeans. Defenders of slavery suggested Africans were innately wild, uncivilized, inferior to whites, and naturally fit for slavery.[5]

The earliest sustained arguments for black inferiority arose in this period. Edward Long, a Jamaican jurist and a plantation owner, and Charles White, an English physician, employed an ancient model of racial (racist!) taxonomy to argue for the natural inferiority of Africans. In the nineteenth century, as abolitionism grew, folk images depicting Indians and blacks as inherently inferior became popular. The scientific writings of Samuel Morton, a Philadelphia physician who collected and measured skulls; Louis Agassiz, a Harvard zoologist; Josiah Nott, an Alabama physician; and others identified the Negro, as black people were called at the time, as "a separate human species." Scientific debates thus emerged in the mid-nineteenth century about the Negro's place in nature. "On one side were polygenists who,

---

[4] Ibid.
[5] Ibid.

using cranial measurements and archaeological measurements, asserted that blacks had been created separately and were a distinct species." Using equally pseudoscientific racism, monogenists argued for a single creation. Yet they maintained Negros had degenerated. Both of these "scientific" perspectives accepted the Negro essentially as a distinct species. These racist classifications became widespread throughout Europe and America during the eighteenth and nineteenth centuries.[6]

The category of race as we use it today in America emanated out of this racist context. Thinkers in the eighteenth and nineteenth centuries basically defined *race* as a series of fixed, immutable, determined, biological character-istics that made a group superior or inferior to other groups without allowing for individual differentiation within a particular group. One aspect of early race theory was the belief that certain races were biologically more beautiful than others. For example, in his *Outline of the History of Mankind*, Christoph Meiners (1747–1816) stated, "One of the chief characteristics of tribes and peoples is the beauty or ugliness of the whole body or face."[7] He classified blacks as "ugly" people distinguished from the "white and beautiful peoples by their sad lack in virtue and their various terrible vices."[8]

Racism is an ideology of hate, particularly directed toward black or dark-skinned people, which seemed to follow logically from these early studies of race. This ideology of hate often has led to a white majority group socially and economically marginalizing black and brown people. This marginaliza-tion has resulted in poverty for many black and brown people and in lack of educational opportunities for them as well. Strictly speaking, *racism* refers to

any attitude towards individuals and groups of people which posits a direct linear connection between physical and mental

---

[6] Ibid.

[7] Benjamin Isaac, *The Invention of Racism in Classical Antiquity* (Princeton: Princeton University Press, 2004), 105.

[8] Christoph Meiners, *Grundiss der Geschichte der Menschheit* (Lengo, 1785), 116.

qualities. It therefore attributes to those individuals and groups of people collective traits, physical, mental, and moral, which are constant and unalterable by human will, because they [are believed by the racist] to be caused by hereditary factors or external influences, such as climate or geography (brackets my emphasis).[9]

One thing that makes racism so evil and potentially deadly is that racists consider individuals "as superior or inferior because they are believed to share imagined physical, mental, and moral attributes with the group to which they are deemed to belong, and it is assumed that they cannot change these traits individually."[10] In the US, the majority group's racist perception of minority groups led to the creation and implementation of laws and policies that socially and economically enslaved black and brown people to the white majority—the impact of which can arguably still be felt in twenty-first-century America and the SBC. A few examples of this impact are economic inequality, educational inequality, and the small, but increasing, minority of black and brown people with power in the SBC.

Many racists in the eighteenth and nineteenth centuries—and many racists today—believed it was impossible for members of a particular race to change their fixed, biological traits because they were predetermined by a race's ontological biology. This is why many of our founding fathers held racist ideas about blacks, why racist Nazis sought to exterminate the Jewish people, why the Ku Klux Klan committed hate crimes against African-Americans and other ethnic minorities, and why many Southern Baptists historically have believed blacks are inferior to whites: these white supremacist groups have historically embraced a white-supremacist view of the world, a view which by definition requires them to classify nonwhite groups as racially inferior based on perceived physical, mental, and moral traits.

---

[9] Isaac, *The Invention of Racism in Classical Antiquity*, 23.
[10] Ibid.

White supremacy (that is, the prioritizing of white people, white culture(s), and white perspectives) has often manifested itself by means of violence and terror—as we've seen with the Nazis, slavery, lynching, Jim Crow laws, the KKK, and recently in the Charleston shooting at Emanuel AME Church. I would argue that the enduring effects of a white-supremacist ideology are still present among Southern Baptists. For example, when Southern Baptist parents refuse to let their kids date or marry Christians of other races, they do so because of an inherited—and maybe even subconscious— white supremacist worldview. White supremacist ideology is the reason certain Southern Baptists ask racist questions like "Why do black people act that way?" A white supremacist worldview may be present when Southern Baptist teachers and professors ignore black and brown scholarship or black or brown contributors to American history. A white supremacist worldview may be present when Southern Baptists suspect black and brown thinkers of being intellectually inferior or theologically suspect. A white supremacist worldview may be present when Southern Baptists uncritically defend the Confederate flag—a symbol of white supremacist, racial hatred toward black and brown people.

A white supremacist worldview may be present when Southern Baptists fail to pursue racial reconciliation in their personal relationships, communities, and churches, or leave their communities or churches when they diversify. A white supremacist worldview may be present when white Southern Baptist leaders do not share, or only grudgingly share, leadership and influence with vetted, qualified, and competent black and brown leaders. A white supremacist worldview is evident when whiteness is appreciated and celebrated, but non-whiteness is denigrated. A white-supremacist worldview may be present when black and brown people are excluded from Southern Baptist conferences and platforms or when their inclusion is limited to addresses on race relations, to breakout sessions, and to preconference sessions—even when black and brown people are more qualified to speak on certain issues than certain white Southern Baptist leaders.

To erase the stain of racism in the SBC requires all racial groups within the denomination to preach reconciliation, to live multiethnic lives, and to reject and fight against the enduring effects of white supremacy with the gospel of the Jewish Messiah, Jesus. The Bible sets forth some steps forward, steps that can help Southern Baptists (and all Christians who have ears to hear!)—especially white Southern Baptists, who are still by far the most dominant, powerful, and privileged racial group in the convention. After my biblical analysis, I provide fifteen exhortations to Southern Baptists with the hope they will stir up the desire for even more genuine multiracial, gospel partnerships within the SBC.

Race, Racism, and Gospel in the Bible

As the above discussion suggests, the category of racial identity has always been a social construct. Yet racial identity both in the biblical world and in the modern world was constructed for different reasons and with different methods. The concept of race was regarded differently in the biblical world than in the modern one. In the biblical material, racial identity is not based on pseudoscience, which wrongly argues one's racial identity is based exclusively on biology. In Deuteronomy 7:1–24, Moses constructs Israel's racial identity based on geographic, theological, and ethical boundaries. These identity markers distinguished Israel's identity from the identities of the other nations. In the Greek translation of the Old Testament, the Septuagint, the translators use the word *genos* to classify nonhuman parts of creation as groups/races/classes/kinds and to classify human beings in different races/groups/classes/kinds. Animals are called a *genos* (race/kind/class/group) separate from other aspects of creation (e.g., LXX Gen 1:11–25). Although the word *genos* is not used in reference to Adam and Eve in the Greek translation of Genesis, God made male and female after his image into a distinct race/kind/group/class of creation (Gen 1:11–31).

In the New Testament, Luke identifies Aquila as a Jew from the *genos* (race/kind/class/group) of Pontus. This suggests geography contributed to one's racial identity from Luke's perspective (Acts 18:2). Both Jew and Pontus are racial categories that focus on different aspects of Aquila's racial identity. In a similar way Luke identifies Apollos as a Jew from the *genos* (race/kind/ group/class) of Alexandria (Acts 18:24). From Luke's perspective Apollos's race was Jewish and Alexandrian. Paul calls Judaism (a movement connected to zealous devotion to the law of Moses) a *genos* (race/kind/class/group) (Gal 1:14). Peter calls Jewish and Gentile Christians a chosen *genos* (race/kind/ group/class) (1 Pet 2:9). Most shockingly, Peter applies to Jewish and Gentile Christians the same racial language that Moses applied to Israel in the Old Testament as he identifies these Christians as a singular race of people (cf. Exod 19:5–6; 1 Pet 2:9).

Thus, the category of race has a broader use in the Bible than in modern terminology. One important distinction is that the biblical category of race was not constructed with pseudoscience for the purpose of establishing a racial hierarchy. Racial categories were employed apart from any consideration of biological inferiority rooted in whiteness or blackness.[11] In fact, Genesis 11:6 in the Septuagint identifies humanity as one *genos* (race/kind/ class/group). The Greek term *ethnos* (nation, Gentile) overlaps with *genos*. Both terms function as racial categories (compare, for example, the above texts with Exod 1:9). The plural term "Gentiles" (*ethnikoi* [Matt 6:7], *ethnē*

---

[11] There is a strong black witness in the Bible. For example, see J. Daniel Hays, *From Every People and Nation: A Biblical Theology of Race* (Downers Grove: InterVarsity Press, 2003). And there are ancient examples where one's racial identity was related to one's blackness. For example, Gay Byron, *Symbolic Blackness and Ethnic Difference in Early Christian Literature: Blackened by Their Sins—Early Christian Ethno-Political Rhetorics about Egyptians, Ethiopians, Blacks, and Blackness* (London: Routledge, 2002). But my point is that race was not fundamentally constructed in the Bible or in antiquity via pseudoscientific racist assumptions about biological inferiorities.

[Matt 28:19]) always refers to non-Jewish people and/or non-Jewish territories in the New Testament—hence, the translation "Gentiles" or "nations" in so many English translations. Contrary to popular opinion,[12] the term *ethnē* in the plural does not refer to people groups as much as it does to non-Jewish groups and/or non-Jewish territories (e.g., Matt 6:32; 12:21; Acts 10:45; 11:1).[13]

If my fellow Southern Baptists want to remove the stain of racism from the SBC, we must admit that racism based on white-supremacist definitions of race still exists in our convention and that such ideas depart from Scripture's teaching on race. We must understand that the Bible's category of race has absolutely nothing to do with racial hierarchy based on biological inferiority.[14] We must also understand that the gospel of Jesus Christ is a message about the vertical reconciliation of Jews and Gentiles to God and a message about the horizontal reconciliation of Jews and Gentiles to one another.

Certain Southern Baptists view racial reconciliation as a social issue instead of a gospel issue because of an incomplete understanding of both the gospel and race. For example, Randy White, a white Southern Baptist, wrote a piece in 2014 titled "The Evangelical Response to Ferguson and Why I Don't Get It."[15] He argued that racial reconciliation is not a gospel issue but rather a social issue. He limited his definition of race to skin color. He

---

[12] The books and sermons are too many to mention.

[13] For examples from the New Testament, see Matt 6:32; 12:21; 25:32; 28:19; Mark 13:10; Luke 12:30; 21:24; Acts 4:25; 10:45; 11:1; 13:19, 46, 48; 14:16; 15:7; 18:6; 21:21; Rom 2:14; 9:30; 15:9–12, 16, 27; 16:26; 1 Cor 12:2; Gal 2:8–9, 14; 3:8, 14; Eph 2:11; 3:6; 4:17; 1 Thess 4:5; 2 Tim 4:17; Rev 11:18; 12:5; 14:8; 15:4; 17:15; 18:3, 23; 19:15; 20:3, 8, 24. For a detailed analysis of *ethnos* and *genos*, see Sechrest, *A Former Jew*.

[14] For my fuller discussion of race, see Jarvis J. Williams, *A Chosen Race and a Royal Priesthood: A Biblical Theology of Ethnic Identity* (Wheaton: Crossway, forthcoming).

[15] For the entire post, see "I Don't Understand the Evangelical Response to Ferguson," Randy White Ministries, accessed July 20, 2016, http://www.randy whiteministries.org/2014/11/26/dont-understand-evangelical-response-ferguson.

strongly criticized certain fellow Southern Baptists for suggesting, in light of the sad events in Ferguson, that the Christian gospel speaks to issues of race and racial reconciliation.

Pastor White seems to understand the gospel only as a vertical message that explains how one becomes a Christian without the horizontal message of racial reconciliation. As a result, he appears to conclude that the gospel has nothing to do with race or racial reconciliation. Thus, when Christians either strongly oppose perceived or actual racial injustice committed against African-Americans and other racial groups or when they contend that racial reconciliation is a gospel issue, Pastor White, and fellow Southern Baptists who share his view, protest by saying that racial reconciliation is either a social issue or maybe an implication of the gospel. But it is certainly not part of the gospel's demand.

On the other hand though some Southern Baptists, even in recent years, have argued racial reconciliation is a "social issue" rather than a "gospel issue,"[16] such a view represents a misunderstanding of the Bible's teaching. Verses like Romans 1:16–17; Galatians 2:11–14; and Ephesians 2:11–3:8 demonstrate that the Bible's categories of race and racial reconciliation intersect with its categories of salvation and gospel. Especially in Ephesians, the mystery of the gospel is defined as the unification of all things in Christ (Eph 1:9–10), which includes the reconciliation of Jews and Gentiles into "one new humanity" (Eph 2:11–3:8 NIV). Paul defines this reconciliation of Jews and Gentiles as the good news of the inexpressible riches of Christ (Eph 2:11–3:10).

Jesus likewise emphasized horizontal elements of the gospel when he asserted that he came to preach the gospel to the poor, oppressed, and captive in fulfillment of Isaiah 61:1(Luke 4:18–19). The Gospel of Luke reveals that Jesus preached as good news that the poor, the sick, the rich, the

---

[16] See, for example, Randy White, "I Don't Understand the Evangelical Response to Ferguson."

marginalized, and any other category of person who repents and follows him (vertical realities) can enter into the kingdom of God, but they must live as a unified people in obedience to King Jesus (horizontal reality), the Savior of all people who repent and follow him (Luke 4:18–13:9). In essence, Jesus preached racial reconciliation as part of his gospel message (Matt 15:21–28; Mark 7:1–37; Eph 2:17).

Southern Baptists who affirm that reconciliation is a gospel issue are on firm biblical grounds. At times, their message is often ambiguous and confusing because what they mean by gospel, race, justice, and racial reconciliation is not clear. And often they do not provide a clear and precise explanation of how race, justice, and racial reconciliation intersect with the gospel. Precise definition of terms is crucial because these concepts are not self-evident.

Southern Baptists' confusion surrounding these issues is illustrated by the fact that some incorrectly teach that the gospel requires churches to be multiethnic. I agree that gospel-centered racial reconciliation produces multiethnic and diverse churches. But ethnic diversity is not the same as gospel-centered racial reconciliation, and the goal of gospel-centered racial reconciliation is not simply diversity. Gospel-centered racial reconciliation is the pursuit of love for the "other" that flows from the Spirit-empowered obedience of those who repent, believe in the cross and resurrection of Jesus by faith, and are justified by faith in Jesus Christ, the Jewish Messiah (Acts 2:1–41; Rom 3:21–4:25; Gal 2:11–6:2). To define racial reconciliation as simply diversity is misleading. Ambiguity about the gospel's horizontal dimension inevitably leads to nebulosity when one promotes racial reconciliation. And this nebulosity makes some Southern Baptists who support gospel-centered racial reconciliation vulnerable to criticism that their proposals sound like a spiritualized version of affirmative action, which is not the same as gospel-centered racial reconciliation.

Southern Baptists need to develop a biblical theology of the gospel, tracing the concept of gospel from the Old Testament to the New Testament. In addition, they must be committed to the whole gospel, emphasizing how the mysterious gospel in the Old Testament has been fulfilled in the death and resurrection of Jesus and now is fully revealed to the church via the Spirit-empowered ministry of the apostles and prophets (Eph 2:11–3:13). The gospel includes both entry language (repentance and faith, justification by faith and reconciliation with God [Rom 3:21–5:11; 1 Cor 15:1–8], etc.) and maintenance language (walking in the Spirit [Gal 5:16–26], reconciliation between Jews and Gentiles [Eph 2:11–3:8], and loving one another in the power of the Spirit [Gal 5:13–14; 6:1–2]). Walking in the Spirit is a gospel reality because Jesus died for our sins to deliver us from this present evil age (Gal 1:4) so that Jews and Gentiles would receive the blessing of Abraham (Gal 3:14a), which is the Spirit (Gal 3:14b). Thus, to walk in the Spirit is to live out the gospel reality of the new, Spirit-empowered age to which the prophets pointed (Isaiah 40–66; Jer 31:31–34; Ezekiel 36–37) and for which Christ died to redeem Jews and Gentiles (Gal 1:4; 3:13–14; 6:16). Because of much confusion among evangelicals about the meaning of the gospel, I further develop below a holistic and complicated definition of the gospel in the most simplistic way I can without compromising the integrity of the argument or the biblical material.

The noun "gospel" (*euaggelion*) and the verb "to announce the gospel/ good news" (*euaggelizō*) should not be defined exclusively in terms of justi-fication by faith. For example, justification by faith is important for Paul's soteriology in Galatians, but Paul's gospel in Galatians includes more than justification by faith. That is, Paul does not use *euaggelion* ("gospel"), *dikaioō* ("to declare to be in the right"), and *dikaisounē* ("righteousness") as synonyms in Galatians. The noun *euaggelion* occurs in pagan literature to refer to the emperor cult. The announcement of a new emperor's birth was *euaggelion* ("gospel/good news").[17] A form of this noun (*euaggelia*) occurs only once in

---

[17] U. Becker, "Gospel," in *Dictionary of New Testament Theology*, ed. Collin Brown (Grand Rapids: Zondervan, 1986), 2:104–14.

the LXX, 2 Kings 4:10 (Hebrew and English 2 Sam 4:10). There it refers to the good report a messenger thought he was giving to David about Saul's death until David seized and killed the messenger. *Euaggelion* occurs numerous times in Galatians to refer to the announcement about Jesus (Gal 1:6–7, 11; 2:2, 5, 7, 14).

The verb *euaggelizō* occurs approximately twenty times in the LXX. It refers to the announcement about the death of Saul (LXX 1 Kgs 31:9—as good news; LXX 2 Kgs 1:20—as bad news; 4:10—as someone thinking Saul's death was good news). It refers to an announcement that God delivered David from his enemies (LXX 2 Kgs 18:19). It refers to an announcement of good news to the king (LXX 2 Kgs 18:26, 31). It refers to the proclamation of good things (LXX 3 Kgs 1:42 = Eng. 1 Kgs 1:42). Jeremiah uses this verb to reference his birth announcement as bad news (LXX Jer 20:15). However, closer parallels to Paul's use of this term in Galatians are places in the LXX where it refers to the announcement of Israel's judgment and salvation.

Euaggelizō refers to the announcement of the Lord's judgment. In LXX Psalm 95, the psalmist praises the Lord for his judging acts. He proclaims that he's a glorious God who will come in judgment against the nations. In LXX Psalm 95:2 (Eng. Ps 96:2), before the psalmist expresses the coming judgment of the Lord against the nations, he exhorts the people of God to praise the Lord and to announce (*euaggelizō*) his salvation. In light of LXX Psalm 95:10 (Eng. Ps 96:10), the announcement of the Lord's salvation is an announcement that the Lord currently reigns as King.

A similar idea occurs in a first-century-BC Jewish work called the Psalms of Solomon 11.[18] The author praises God for his faithfulness, petitions the Lord to keep being faithful, and exhorts Israel to be holy. In Psalms of Solomon 11:1, the psalmist urges the people to announce in Jerusalem

---

[18] The Psalms of Solomon are included in a collection of writings known as the Pseudepigrapha. This collection is not Scripture, but these psalms shine a bright ray of light onto the vocabulary used in the New Testament.

(*euaggelizomenou*) that God has been merciful to Israel by watching over the nation.

Euaggelizō refers to the announcement of the Lord's salvation and the promise of the Spirit in the LXX Joel. There Joel 3:5 connects God's salvation with the announcement (*euaggelizō*) of his salvation (i.e., the announcement of good news). Joel warns that the Lord will come in judgment (LXX Joel 2:1–17) and then announces the Lord's promise of salvation for his people (LXX Joel 2:18–3:2). This announcement includes the promise of the Spirit and is followed by another announcement that God will come in judgment (LXX Joel 3:3–4) and that everyone who calls out to the Lord will be saved (LXX Joel 3:5), just as the Lord promised. Joel states that the one who is saved and those who announce (*euaggelizomenou*) this salvation will be survivors in Jerusalem and Zion.

Euaggelizō refers to the announcement of the Lord's judgment of the nations in the LXX. The minor prophetic book Nahum is an oracle of judgment against Nineveh. The oracle begins with both the prophet's announcement of the Lord's judgment (LXX Nah 1:1–6) and with the announcement that he shows mercy to those who seek their refuge in him (LXX Nah 1:7). Before Nahum promises Israel that the Lord will destroy his enemies (LXX Nah 1:8–14; 2:1–3:19), Nahum urges the people to see upon the mountains (i.e., above the destruction that will fall on Nineveh and on all of the Lord's adversaries) the feet of the one who announces (*euaggelizō*) good news (LXX Nah 2:1). This announcement is the good news that the Lord will save Judah from his judgment, which he has reserved for Nineveh and all his enemies.

LXX Isaiah is especially helpful for understanding Paul's use of *euaggelizō* in Galatians since he directly quotes and alludes to Isaiah throughout the letter. In LXX Isaiah *euaggelizō* refers to the announcement of Israel's salvation in the midst of the Lord's judgment. In LXX Isaiah 40:9; 52:7; 60:6; and 61:1, this verb refers to the announcement of the Lord's salvation of Israel. In LXX Isaiah 40:9, Israel is exhorted to get on a high mountain to announce this salvation (cf. LXX Nah 2:1). In LXX Isaiah 52:7, the Lord himself announces to Israel and the nations the good news of Israel's salvation and that he reigns over her. His message of salvation stands in authority over those upon whom he promises to bring judgment. The bearer of this announcement (i.e., the good news of salvation from judgment) is described as beautiful because he brings a message of salvation in the midst of his announcement of judgment. The announcement of salvation is a promise that the Lord will deliver from his destruction those who hear his announcement of salvation and judgment and believe in the promise of salvation. In LXX Isaiah 60:6, the nations announce Israel's salvation. In LXX Isaiah 61:1, the Lord anoints someone with his Spirit to announce the good news of salvation (cf. Luke 4:18–19). This announcement comes to Israel as the prophet Isaiah pronounces her imminent judgment in the form of exile. Alongside the announcement of a future exile for Israel, the Lord gives the nation good news of salvation.

In summary, in each of the above examples, *euaggelizō* is connected with the announcement of the Lord's mercy or salvation, and the Lord himself is present in the announcement. This means the heralds of the announcement are not simply proclaiming what the Lord will do for his people or what he will do against his enemies, but they also proclaim the Lord himself. When the gospel of the Lord is announced, the Lord himself is present in the announcement in order to effect both the salvation and the judgment the announcement proclaims. Thus, the verb *euaggelizō* refers to the act of announcing the message of salvation and judgment in the LXX. The noun *euaggelion* refers to the content of the announcement. But does the preceding analysis hold true in the New Testament? I only have space to give examples from Galatians.

The verb and the noun in Galatians carry the same force and convey the same idea as in the LXX. In Galatians *euaggelion* refers to the report/announcement about Jesus: he is the Lord and Messiah who fulfills God's promises of salvation. These promises of salvation include new creation, justification by faith, and the ushering in of the age of the Spirit.

The noun *euaggelion* occurs seven times in Galatians (1:6–7, 11; 2:2, 5, 7, 14). The verb *euaggelizō* occurs six times in Galatians (1:8–9, 11, 16, 23; 4:13). Paul's use of *euaggelion* and *euaggelizō* depends both on Isaiah 40–66, since Paul alludes to or quotes Isaiah throughout the letter, and the context of his argument in Galatians. Paul links the gospel vocabulary in Galatians with themes of salvation from Isaiah 40–66. Of course, a biblical definition of gospel must go beyond simply analyzing these two words. One must also analyze the numerous gospel concepts in the Old Testament, developed within Second Temple Judaism and redefined in light of the cross and resurrection of Jesus in the New Testament.

When one carefully reads Isaiah and Galatians beside each other, one should see that Paul and Isaiah offer many components of gospel. They mention the redemption of sinners from the present evil age (cf. Gal 1:4 and 3:13 with Isa 44:21; 53:1–12). They mention new creation (cf. Gal 6:15 with Isa 65:17–25). They discuss righteous living/righteousness in the new covenant by means of the power of the Spirit (cf. Gal 5:16–24 with Isa 56:1–5; 60:1–22). They mention the promise of a spiritualized Jerusalem who will be set free from spiritual slavery in the messianic age as opposed to a physical Jerusalem that will be a slave under Torah during the messianic age (cf. Gal 4:21–27 with Isa 54:1–17). They affirm the promise of universal salvation of Jews and Gentiles who have faith by means of the Messiah/Servant (cf. Gal 2:11–3:29 with Isa 49:1–26; 52:13–53:12). They speak to the importance of hearing the report/message about salvation and the importance of receiving it by faith (cf. Gal 3:2–3 with Isa 52:7; 53:1).

In Galatians 3:8, Paul uses another word for "announce/preach the good news" (*proeuaggelizomai*), which only appears here in extant Greek from the biblical tradition. Paul uses this verb to refer to the Scripture's preaching/ announcing the gospel beforehand to Abraham when it proclaimed that all nations would be blessed in him (cf. Gal 3:8 with Gen 12:3). This blessing comes to the nations because God promised to justify the Gentiles by faith (Gal 3:8). So, with the citations of Genesis 12:3 and 15:6 in Galatians 3, Paul indicates that the gospel and the announcement of the good news in Galatians include justification by faith. Furthermore, we see that the background behind Paul's meaning for "gospel/announce the good news" should not be limited to Isaiah 40–66 and includes the Abrahamic promises of land, seed, and universal blessing in Genesis 12–50. Paul understands these promises to Abraham, which were gospel promises, to be reiterated in Isaiah 40–66 and to be fulfilled in Jesus, the Messiah/Servant and the promised seed of Abraham (Gal 3:16). These observations are supported by the parallel themes of salvation in Isaiah and Galatians, by the connections between Isaiah 40–66 and Genesis 12–50 (e.g., universal salvation, divine blessing to the nations), and by Paul's reference to Jesus as the true descendant of Abraham, as the One in whom the Abrahamic promises find their fulfillment, and as the One in whom the promises of salvation in Isaiah 40–66 find their fulfillment (Gal 3:1–6:15).

Based on the above analysis, several concluding observations are necessary. First, the gospel in Galatians should not be defined only as justification by faith—though Galatians teaches justification is part (an important part) of Paul's gospel, a part from which the Galatians were in danger of turning away. Second, the chief problem described in Galatians is that Paul's opponents were making Torah obedience necessary for Gentile Christians to be part of the people of God (2:11–14; 5:2–6; 6:13). Paul argues that a Torah-observant and Gentile-exclusive announcement is contrary to the announcement of good news he received from Jesus Christ and God the Father, who raised him from the dead (Gal 1:1, 6–9, 11–12). His announcement of good news is both identical to and the fulfillment of the announcement in Isaiah 40–66 and Genesis 12–50. Third, when the Galatian churches first encountered the words *euaggelion* and *euaggelizō* in Galatians 1:6–11 as they heard this letter read in a worship context, I do not believe they thought Paul was referencing only a turn from justification by faith to a false gospel. Their understanding of *euaggelion* and *euaggelizō* would have included justification by faith as well as, at minimum, the other gospel/salvation themes occurring in the letter that parallel Isaiah 40–66 and Genesis 12–50. Paul likely proclaimed these themes to them during his visit with them (cf. Acts 13:13–14:23 with Gal 5:20–21).[19]

These conclusions have strong support in Galatians. In Galatians 1:6–2:14, Paul uses the gospel vocabulary without mentioning justification. In Galatians 1:6–9, he references his shock that the Galatians were turning away to another gospel (*euaggelion*) and says the apostolic curse falls upon all who make such a turn. In Galatians 1:16, Paul talks about his call to preach the gospel (*euggelizō*) to the Gentiles. In Galatians 2:11–14, Paul says Peter failed to walk in the truth of the gospel when he withdrew from table fellowship with Gentile Christians, for fear of the Jews, after men from James arrived. Peter believed all the right things about justification by faith for Jews, but he departed from the gospel by imposing Jewish legal demands on Gentile Christians. His error stemmed from an incorrect view of the gospel's horizontal component.

Hence, Paul reminds Peter in Galatians 2:15–21 that Jews and Gentiles are justified the same way and that they enter into the people of God the same way: by faith in Jesus Christ apart from works of law. When Paul condemned Peter as accursed in Galatians 2:11, he placed Peter under both the apostolic curse and the Deuteronomic curse because he was advocating a Torah-observant, Gentile-exclusive gospel. Paul's gospel, instead, announced that Jesus died for those under Torah's curse to extend to them the blessing of Abraham (Gal 3:10–14) and to deliver them from the present evil age (Gal 1:4). And Paul speaks of the Deuteronomic curse coming upon those who are under Torah and who do not walk in the power of the Spirit because

---

[19] This statement assumes a southern Galatian theory. For further discussion on this, see Jarvis J. Williams, *Commentary on Galatians*, NCCS, edited by Mike Bird and Craig Kenner (Eugene, OR: Cascade Books, forthcoming 2017).

they will not inherit the kingdom of God (Gal 5:16–21). The point to not miss here is that Paul uses gospel vocabulary more than once in Galatians 1–2 prior to his discussion of justification by faith in Galatians 2:16.

In Paul's view, one can conceptually confirm justification by faith and yet still stand condemned by the gospel (e.g., Peter [Gal 2:11–14]) if he does not walk in the Spirit (Gal 5:16–22), but instead fulfills the lusts of the flesh (Gal 5:16–22). Furthermore, my view finds added support outside of Galatians when one considers the number of times the noun *euaggelion* ("gospel") and/or the verb *euaggelizō* ("I announce the good news") occur without a reference to justification by faith. In 1 Corinthians 15:1–8, Paul discusses the gospel he preached to the Corinthians and the gospel by which they were saved without mentioning justification by faith. Instead, Paul mentions the cross and the resurrection as a summary of his gospel. This observation acknowledges that justification is only one of the many important parts of the gospel.

Based on the evidence in Galatians, we can perhaps define *euaggelion* and *euaggelizō* in Galatians as the proclamation/announcement of God's promises of salvation revealed in the Old Testament and fulfilled in Jesus Christ. A more technical way of saying this would be that the gospel in Galatians is the announcement of God's redemptive work in and through Christ for the salvation of sinners in fulfillment of God's Old Testament promises of salvation for Jews and Gentiles. This redemptive work in Galatians includes, but should not be limited to, the following: (1) the death of Jesus as a substitute to deliver Jews and Gentiles from the present evil age and from the curse of the law (Gal 1:4; 3:13), (2) God's resurrection of Jesus from the dead (Gal 1:1), (3) justification by faith alone in Christ alone apart from Torah obedience/becoming Jewish (Gal 2:15–21), (4) deliverance from the curse of the Mosaic law as the badge of covenant membership by means of the fulfillment of the Abrahamic covenant through Jesus, Abraham's promised descendant (Gal 3:1–29), (5) the reception of the Spirit by faith because of Jesus's death and resurrection (Gal 3:2–5, 10–14), (6) Abrahamic sonship

(Gal 3:6–4:7), (7) the ability and freedom to live in pursuit of love in the power of the Spirit to thereby fulfill the entire law (Gal 4:21–5:26), (8) new creation (Gal 6:15), and (9) membership in God's new Israel for those who have identified with Jesus Christ by faith (Gal 6:10, 16).[20]

Racial Division and Reconciliation in the Bible

Scripture supports the notion that racial division is a universal power that rules and reigns like an evil tyrant over all Jews and Gentiles because of the historic fall of Adam and Eve in the garden of Eden (Genesis 3–4; 11; Rom 5:12–6:23). Adam and Eve were part of the human race (Gen 11:6). Their transgression resulted in both a vertical (Genesis 3) and a horizontal curse of the entire cosmos (Genesis 4). The vertical curse separated humans from God, and the horizontal curse separated them and their offspring from one another, evident by Cain's murder of his brother Abel in Genesis 4. This murder represents the first violent and hostile act among humans in the Bible.

Because of Adam's and Eve's transgression (Genesis 3), Cain's desire to perform a violent act against a fellow member of the human race existed in his heart before he murdered his brother. As God stated in Genesis 3:15, hostility would result between the seed of the woman and the seed of the serpent. The narrative of Genesis 3–4 immediately shows this enmity, with Eve's seed (Abel) and the serpent's seed (Cain) at enmity with each other. The internal hostility in Cain's heart was one reason God exhorted him to master his sin. His sin was crouching at his door, eager to seize him (Gen 4:6–7). Yet the Bible teaches that Jesus, the new Adam, died and rose from the dead to kill all forms of sin and to reverse the vertical and horizontal curse over the entire cosmos by restoring vertical and horizontal relationships (John 1:29;

---

[20] Of course, for an exhaustive definition of gospel, one must look at the whole Bible—a project outside the purview of this chapter. But may what I have put forth above put to rest once and for all one-sided, incomplete, and misleading definitions of the gospel.

Rom 3:25; 5:12–21; 15:8–21; Gal 2:11–3:29; 6:16; Eph 2:11–3:8; 5:16–26; Col 1:19–22; Rev 21:1–22:5).

The horizontal curse brings us to the topic of racial division. Paul generalizes racial division as Jewish and Gentile division in a few of his letters. He calls the Ephesians "Gentiles in the flesh" (Eph 2:11).[21] Yet racial division between Jews and Gentiles in the Old Testament and continuing in the New Testament was based on Torah, not on the color of skin. Jews and Gentiles came in all shapes, colors, and sizes in the ancient world. For example, Gentiles describe the complexions of other Gentiles in numerous ancient texts.[22] "Gentiles" (*ethnē*) were separated from the commonwealth of Israel when they were dead in transgressions and sins prior to their association with Jesus, the Jewish Messiah, because they were not Jewish (Eph 2:1–11). As descendants of Abraham, the Jewish people received circumcision as the sign of participation in the Abrahamic covenant (Gen 17:10–14). Without this sign, Gentiles were racially separated from God's promises to Abraham to be fulfilled through Israel's Messiah (Eph 2:11). This sign eventually became part of the Mosaic covenant (Lev 12:3; Jos 5:2–9).

Ephesians 2:12 affirms this interpretation with the words "without Christ," "alienated from the commonwealth of Israel," "strangers of the covenants of promise," "without hope," "and those living without God in the world." Gentiles were separated from God's promises of salvation to Israel, God's covenant people (Rom 3:1–2; 9:4–5; 11:1–2; Phil 3:4–6), separated from access to God's messianic promises given to Israel in the Old Testament (2 Sam 7:11–13; Psalms 2; 110), separated from God's covenantal promises made to Abraham regarding land, seed, and a universal blessing (Gen 12:1–4; 13:14–18; 15:1–21; 17:1–21; Eph 2:11–12), separated from the promises to David regarding a descendant to reign over his kingdom forever (2 Sam 7:12–17; 23:5; Ps 89:3, 27–37, 49), and separated from the

---

[21] Unless otherwise indicated, all translations of biblical texts are mine.

[22] For example, Gay, *Symbolic Blackness and Ethnic Difference.*

promises to Israel and Judah regarding a future restoration (Jer 31:31–34; Ezekiel 36–37).

Sin vertically alienated humanity from God and horizontally from one another (Gen 3:15). However, the law further divided Jews and Gentiles from each other when it entered history, not because the law was evil or promoted legalism but because the law revealed a knowledge of sin (Rom 4:15; 5:13; 7:1–25; Gal 3:19) and because it served as a dividing wall between the children of the covenant (Jews) and those who were outside the covenant (Gentiles). In Ephesians 2:14–16, Paul describes the law as a dividing wall, a fence, hostility, and a source of enmity between Jews and Gentiles. Yes, God's covenantal promises anticipated the inclusion of the Gentiles from the beginning (Gen 12:1–13; Isa 42:6–9; 49:6; 60:1–3). Moreover, Paul stated that Jews would receive those promises only by means of faith in Jesus Christ (Rom 9:1–5; 9:30–10:13; Gal 2:11–5:1). However, Jews at least had an ethnic connection with the Jewish Messiah and with God's promises to Jews and Gentiles (Gen 49:10; Deut 18:15; 2 Sam 7:12–13; Psalm 2; 45:3–5, 17; Isaiah 40–66), unlike the Gentiles (Rom 2:14).

Paul states in Ephesians that God accomplished reconciliation for Jews and Gentiles. Paul asserts that Gentiles were brought near God's promises of salvation to Jews "by the blood of Christ Jesus" (Eph 2:13). Paul interprets Isaiah 9:6; 52:7; and 57:19 in light of the death and resurrection of Jesus Christ to emphasize this reconciliation (Eph 2:13–18; cf. 1:15–23). "Peace" in Ephesians 2:14 and the proclamation of peace to "those far off" and "to those near" in Ephesians 2:17 link 2:13–18 with Isaiah. The proclamation of peace in Ephesians 2:17 is a reference to the proclamation of the gospel. In Isaiah 9:6, "peace" refers to the Jewish Messiah. In Isaiah 52:7 and 57:19, "peace" refers to the salvation (i.e., the good news) that Yahweh promised to bring to Israel through the Jewish Messiah. According to Ephesians 2:13–16, the good news of the gospel is that the Jewish Messiah, Jesus, died so that he would abolish the dividing wall of hostility (i.e., the law of Moses) between Jews and Gentiles, so that he would reconcile Jews and Gentiles to God and to each other, and so that he would create Jews and Gentiles into one new man, into one body through the cross. By means of Jesus's death (Eph 2:13, 16) and resurrection and exaltation (Eph 1:15–23), God recreated Jews and Gentiles into one dwelling place of God, in whom the Spirit dwells (Eph 2:18–22). And Jesus himself provided the model for this racial reconciliation in that he preached this gospel of peace (i.e., reconciliation) to Jews near the promises and to Gentiles far away from those promises (Matt 15:21–28).

Racial Reconciliation and the Mystery of the Gospel

The mystery of the gospel is an important theme in Ephesians (Eph 1:9–10). Paul defines this mystery as the unification of all things in Christ (Eph 1:10) and "the gospel of your salvation" (Eph 1:13). As I stated above, evangelicals in general and Southern Baptists in particular often narrowly (and wrongly!) define gospel only in terms of entry language (i.e., how one becomes a Christian). But the gospel is broader than some are willing to admit. It includes both entry language (how one becomes a Christian) and maintenance language (how one lives in Spirit-empowered obedience). Its entry language tells one how to enter the believing community by faith (Rom 3:21–4:25; Gal 2:15–21). Its maintenance language tells one how to live out, in the power of the Spirit, the reality of what God has done for him in Christ (Gal 5:16–6:10; Eph 2:11–6:20). One can also say the gospel is the announcement of God's fulfilling his promises of salvation, which include new creation for Jews and Gentiles in Jesus, the Messiah (e.g., Rom 1:3–4, 16–17; Gal 2:11–6:17).

In Ephesians 2:11–22, Paul argues that the gospel (which, in Ephesians, is the unification of all things in Christ) includes the reconciliation of Jews and Gentiles (different groups) into one new humanity. Paul calls this unification of all things in Christ the mystery (Eph 1:9), the message of truth (Eph 1:13), and the gospel of our salvation (Eph 1:13). Ephesians

3:2 refers to the stewardship of God's grace given to Paul. Ephesians 3:3 describes that stewardship as a mystery made known to Paul by divine revelation—likely a reference to his Damascus road vision (Acts 9; Gal 1:15–16). Ephesians 3:4 further describes this mystery as the mystery of Christ. Ephesians 3:5 states that the mystery was revealed to Paul by the Spirit. Ephesians 3:6 explicitly states the content of the mystery is Jew and Gentile inclusion as equal participants in and equal heirs of God's promises of salvation for the world by means of Jesus, the Jewish Messiah, through the gospel (see also Gal 3:1–4:11). Ephesians 3:8 connects racial reconciliation to the gospel by stating that God graciously called Paul to proclaim as good news the incalculable riches of Christ to the Gentiles. The incalculable riches of Christ refer to the totality of what God has done in Christ for Jews and Gentiles to unify all things in Christ (Eph 1:3–3:21). This unification includes racial reconciliation insofar as race refers to Jews and Gentiles (Eph 2:11–22).

Numerous other passages in the New Testament strongly affirm that Jesus, the Son of God, came to this world as a Jewish man to create a reconciled community comprised of different categories of people. In Luke 4:18–19, Jesus read Isaiah 61:1–2 in a synagogue. The text emphasized that God's Spirit-anointed prophet would come to preach as good news (i.e., gospel) liberty to the captives and the recovering of sight to the blind for the purpose of setting free those who are oppressed. After reading this text, Jesus boldly stated to those in attendance that he was in fact the Promised One from Isaiah 61:1–2. Jesus supported this claim throughout Luke by ministering to both the socially marginalized (e.g., sick people [Luke 5:12–26] and sexually promiscuous women [Luke 7:36–50]) as well as the social elite (e.g., a Roman centurion's servant [Luke 7:1–10] and a tax collector [Luke 19:1–10]). He summoned all groups to repent, believe the gospel, and become part of one reconciled community devoted to him (Mark 1:15; Luke 1:39–2:32; cf. Matthew 5–7).

Fifteen Concluding Exhortations

The Bible provides no direct one-to-one correlation between the reconciliation of Jews and Gentiles to God and to one another and the need to erase the stain of racism from the SBC. Yet the Bible's teaching of reconciliation in Christ certainly applies to the racist past and present struggle with race relations in the SBC. Positively, I applaud and praise God for the progress that has been made on race relations in the SBC. My personal story should make clear that I believe racial reconciliation is in fact happening in many aspects of SBC life. For example, Pastor Fred Luter served two terms as the first African-American president of the SBC. What's more, twenty-three other Baptist state conventions have elected non-Anglo presidents. All these presidential elections are miraculous and exemplify progress! In addition, I currently serve as an associate professor of New Testament interpretation at the oldest school—the School of Theology—of the SBC's flagship seminary. At one time I would not have been able to study at Southern Seminary because of my race. But not only am I the institution's first and only (to my knowledge) four-time graduate; I am also the only African-American New Testament scholar teaching at any Southern Baptist seminary or any Baptist college that cooperates with a state Baptist convention within the SBC family—further evidence of progress!

I applaud the many white Southern Baptists who responded with outcries for justice after the controversial deaths of black men at the hands of predominately white police officers in Ferguson, Staten Island, Baltimore, and elsewhere. Various pastors in the SBC and beyond have courageously risked their own ministries because of the race issue by engaging in discussions about race after controversies surrounding the aforementioned deaths erupted. I further commend all Southern Baptists who speak intelligently and thoughtfully about matters pertaining to race, the gospel, justice, and racial reconciliation. I am especially thankful for white pastors who have partnered with black and brown pastors in the urban context, sacrificing their own ministries and white privileged status within the SBC as a result. However, I think every aspect of Southern Baptist life can do much better on race relations. Therefore, in the rest of this chapter, I offer Southern Baptists (and anyone else who has ears to hear!) fifteen concluding exhortations related to removing the stain of racism from the SBC.

1. Southern Baptists should be quick to listen and slow to speak on race when they do not understand the issues. White supremacy and racism are complicated issues. These issues relate to concepts such as racialization, critical race theory, mass incarceration, economic inequality, educational inequality, and other forms of systemic injustice. Speaking ignorantly about these issues is inappropriate. Southern Baptists, especially white Southern Baptists with privilege and without personal experience of the challenges associated with being a black or brown person in the US, should spend more time listening to their black and brown brothers and sisters instead of trying to speak to, at, about, or for them.

2. Southern Baptists must pray for and support multiethnic church plants in their cities and communities if their churches are not going to pursue reconciliation.

3. Southern Baptists must stop making excuses for why our denomination still has the stain of racism. Many black, brown, and white people in the SBC suffer severely from racial reconciliation exhaustion. We know firsthand how difficult it is to erase the stain of racism with the bleach of the gospel from churches and from a denomination that was founded because of white supremacy. Nevertheless, the gospel calls us as Southern Baptists to work harder at erasing the stain than our racist forebears worked to stain our denomination with white supremacy. These efforts will come at great cost, something many black and brown Southern Baptists have known for some time (and more white Southern Baptists are beginning to realize). Loss of denominational privilege, fewer or zero invitations to speak at Southern Baptist conferences, and racist verbal attacks will inevitably come

to Southern Baptists who work to remove the stain of racism. But we should not make excuses.

4. Southern Baptists must stop limiting the racial reconciliation discussion to the black versus white divide in our convention (Eph 2:1–22), although this divide is significant. This exhortation might seem hypocritical to some given the imbalanced ethnic makeup of this book. But I contend there are many gifted and underrepresented minority groups in Southern Baptist life from whom our white/Anglo-American brothers and sisters can learn. Many diverse brothers and sisters feel just as voiceless as many African-American brothers and sisters in Southern Baptist life.

5. The movement of gospel-centered racial reconciliation within the SBC does not need an African-American savior, an Asian savior, a Latino savior, or a white savior. But we need a multiracial partnership of churches working together in our convention and our communities to advance the gospel of racial reconciliation and to erase the stain of racism from our denomination. This multiracial partnership means my white Southern Baptist brothers and sisters with leadership and influence must share more of both with underrepresented scholars, qualified pastors, and church leaders of color who have thought long about and worked hard to understand complicated issues related to the gospel, race, racial reconciliation, justice, and other important matters facing the SBC. As a racial minority in Southern Baptist life, I have observed that many of our key leaders are white. And when a crisis arises in our convention, our white leaders are often the spokespersons for our denomination or to our churches—even if the crisis that emerges more directly affects minority communities within the SBC.

In my view, if we as Southern Baptists are going to take serious strides toward leading the evangelical world in the work of gospel-centered racial reconciliation in the twenty-first century and toward removing the stain of racism from the SBC, we must listen to and include more qualified, underrepresented voices of color within our denomination. Vetted black and brown people need a platform on which to speak and from which to write about important issues affecting our churches and denomination. Many of the minorities without a voice in denominational life are vetted and have multiple degrees from a variety of academic institutions. And a few of us are published in high-level academic presses and journals while also having proven track records of faithful gospel ministry. But too often we are overlooked for less qualified, nonvetted, less published, and less gifted white brothers and sisters who have privilege within the SBC by virtue of their whiteness and who have access to privileged people within the SBC who share their whiteness.

Some of the issues facing Southern Baptists uniquely affect black and brown people (e.g., systemic and racial injustice). Black and brown Southern Baptists need a platform on which to talk about these issues. But their platform should not be limited to minority audiences within the SBC or to race-related issues. Black and brown Southern Baptists should be heard in other venues of SBC life besides Black Church Week, the committees tasked with addressing racial diversity, and denominational preconferences. Shared leadership within the SBC would perhaps help our denomination gain great insights from the diversity within it and provide credibility with both majority and minority Christians.

6. Southern Baptists need to enlarge their ethnic circles to include more black and brown believers. If Southern Baptists live monoethnic lives, then they will have a limited monoethnic perspective of the complexity of Southern Baptist life.

7. Southern Baptists must recognize that black and brown people can minister to white people and teach them many things about many subjects, including race. Ignorance of black and brown perspectives will only reinforce racist biases.

8. Southern Baptists must understand that black and brown Southern Baptists need white allies in the work of gospel ministry. We want our white

brothers and sisters to share their leadership and influence with qualified black and brown people. I shake my head in despair, confusion, and frustration when certain qualified and articulate black and brown Southern Baptist preachers or scholars appear to be snubbed by the leaders in the SBC when they create speakers' lists for the many influential SBC conferences.

Many conferences in the SBC are filled with predominately white speakers even when a diverse array of qualified black and brown speakers is available. Here's a thought: why doesn't the SBC have a conference on abortion, the gospel, homosexuality, the family, or any other issue with a speakers' list of all black and brown people or a predominate number of black and brown people? If the stain of racism is going to become less apparent within the SBC, white leaders responsible for organizing conferences must intentionally include black and brown people at the center of their conferences. And the SBC needs to have conferences that are predominately led by black and brown individuals. This can help Southern Baptists see that black and brown people lead in our convention too.

9. Southern Baptists must understand that the kingdom of God does not revolve around whiteness or blackness or brownness. Jesus died for many black and brown and red and yellow and white people with strange names and curious accents. God is using many black and brown people to advance the gospel in some of the most difficult places in the world to different races of people. This is one reason Southern Baptists must not suggest with the images they show to promote international missions that white folks are the only ones taking the gospel to these dark places, which usually have large populations with black and brown skin. The last time I read the New Testament, paganism was both in Greece, where the population was light skinned, and Egypt, where the population was dark skinned. Furthermore, Southern Baptist churches need to erase, take down, or paint over all images of a white Jesus, white disciples, and all-white children learning at the feet of Jesus. These images perpetuate white supremacy and suggest the kingdom of God revolves around whiteness.

The same point should be made about the numerous church children's curricula with images of all-white children and a white Jesus with white disciples. These images devalue the various colors God created and make black- or brown-skinned children feel unwelcome, not to mention confused. I was in my twenties before I finally realized Jesus was not white because when I was a child, Bible teachers always showed me images of a white Jesus with white disciples. I have preached in numerous Southern Baptist churches that believe in the mythological white Jesus but are unaware of the historical Jewish Jesus from Nazareth. I blame this on white supremacy.

10. Southern Baptists must recognize that whiteness is not normal and everything else abnormal. Normalcy is in the eye of the beholder—in this case the white majority group within the SBC. Neither the vast majority of the world's population nor the vast majority of those who still need to hear and respond to the gospel are middle-class white Americans. The US is becoming increasingly black and brown. This means if Southern Baptist churches want to be culturally effective, relevant, and credible as we move forward, the SBC and predominantly white Southern Baptist churches desperately need to incorporate more black and brown people into their leadership, when possible.

11. Southern Baptists should not claim they view all people in a color-blind fashion. When Christians deny that they see black, brown, or white skin, they appear to ignore the fact that many black and brown people have suffered much because of the color of their skin at the hands of certain white people in the SBC. And when Christians deny that skin color currently plays a role in determining who assumes leadership and privilege within the SBC, they make the stain of racism more difficult to remove by denying what seems obvious to many black, brown, and white Southern Baptists. Racial progress will not happen in the SBC by denying the obvious. Black, brown, white, and everyone else in the SBC must acknowledge our differences and pursue love, unity, and reconciliation in the gospel in spite of them.

12. Southern Baptists must not play the race card just to serve their political agendas, to get television appearances, to increase Twitter followers, to gain more friends on Facebook, or to get invites to the big white or black and brown conferences. It's easy for white Southern Baptists to be pro-black and pro-brown or in favor of reconciliation and diversity at the big conferences. Or at conferences on race after clear examples of racial injustice occur in the culture. Or when there is debate about removing a racist symbol from the grounds of a state capitol. But racial reconciliation is difficult when a Southern Baptist's child says he wants to marry someone of another race who loves Jesus. Reconciliation is likewise difficult when Southern Baptists with leadership and influence are asked to share those privileges with more qualified black or brown people.

13. If Southern Baptists want to gain credibility in black and brown contexts on matters of gospel reconciliation, they must befriend black and brown people lacking celebrity status. I have observed in my twenty years of being a Southern Baptist that Southern Baptists often are guilty of idolatry because they love to affirm black and brown celebrity Christians. Such affirmation enables white Southern Baptists to maintain their privileged status within the SBC with little sacrifice. White Southern Baptists serious about reconciliation should befriend black and brown people within the SBC who are voiceless and marginalized.

14. Southern Baptists must recognize that the evangelical movement generally and the SBC specifically still lack credibility with many black and brown communities in part because of their historic failure to do the things mentioned above. And they must recognize that many black and brown people continue to question the sincerity of the SBC and evangelicals generally on race relations.

15. Black and brown Southern Baptists are not off the hook. We have an important role to play in removing the stain of racism from the SBC too. We must recognize that just as the white majority in the SBC must

share leadership and influence with us, we must be willing to sacrifice ethnic privileges and preferences when white brothers and sisters enter black and brown spaces. Black and brown Southern Baptists should not ask white Southern Baptists to be more inclusive on the one hand if we are unwilling, on the other hand, to do the same in black and brown spaces within the SBC where we have influence and leadership. Because of sin's universal power and because of racism's prevalence in society, black and brown people have the sin of racism in their hearts too. Black and brown Southern Baptist churches need to become more diverse and inclusive as well. The message of racial reconciliation in the gospel is a universal message for all people throughout the world who claim the name of Jesus Christ. If the stain of racism in the SBC is to become less apparent, then all evangelicals must intentionally and rigorously do their parts in working to remove that stain.

The stain of racism remains in many Southern Baptist pulpits and churches, although they have made much progress. Jesus, our Jewish Savior, has purchased some from every tribe, tongue, people, and nation (Rev 5:9). Southern Baptists need the partnership of all churches committed to our Jewish Savior to fulfill this Great Commission task of gospel-centered racial reconciliation (Matt 28:19–20). Removing the stain of racism from our churches might seem like an impossible task in light of our troubled history. But if red and yellow, black and white, rich and poor Southern Baptists work together in unity to kill racism with the power of the gospel and if churches plant gospel-centered multiethnic churches in the US, the stain of racism will become less apparent in the SBC until the day Jesus returns to redeem Southern Baptists (and all Christians) once and for all from our troubled past and create a perfectly reconciled future in the new heavens and the new earth (Revelation 21–22). Until that day, may Southern Baptist churches in every generation make daily efforts to erase the stain of racism from the SBC!

CHAPTER 4

Theological Steps Toward Removing the Stain of Racism from the Southern Baptist Convention

Walter R. Strickland II

The Conversation

In November of 2012, I attended the annual meeting of the Evangelical Theological Society (ETS) as a bright-eyed first-year PhD student. ETS draws evangelical professors, seminary and college administrators, and independent scholars from a variety of denominational backgrounds. The gathering features theologically rigorous presentations on the most pressing issues of the day. Each year this gathering draws numerous Southern Baptist thinkers and is an occasion for a family reunion of sorts.

Informal conversations at ETS often venture into the content of each scholar's current writing projects or research. These discussions are opportunities to engage new concepts and are a sneak peek into books, articles, and curriculum that will be publicly consumed in the months ahead. In a dialogue with a high-ranking administrator of a Southern Baptist seminary,

I was asked the inevitable question, "What are you currently researching and writing about?" As a student writing a dissertation, I began to explain that I was writing about the relationship between theology and culture among three African-American theologians at the end of the Civil Rights Movement. The typical response to hearing of someone's research is an excited affirmation via asking questions that probe deeper into the subject matter or expressed excitement about the upcoming contribution to scholarship and the church. The response I received was disappointing. Instead the administrator responded, "When are you going to do 'real' theology, and what will you write about when you do so?"

In my development as a theologian, my dissertation was more than a paper to complete a degree; in my mind it validated the ability of African-Americans to think with a Christian worldview about issues that affect us. The administrator's response sent me into a tailspin because it denied the importance of thinking "Christianly" about the African-American experience and caused me to question my acceptance among my denominational family. The interaction drove me to ask: on what grounds does this well-established thinker claim that my project is not real theology? Intertwined in the answer to this question is the solution for removing the racial stain from theology in the Southern Baptist Convention (SBC).

The Explanation

The task of theology is to reflect on God, his Word, and his world for the purpose of knowing, loving, and glorifying him by participating in his mission. Said differently, theology is a dynamic process that integrates "thus saith the Lord" with day-to-day life. Each Christian undertakes the theological task from a specific cultural context; this cultural context produces theological inquiries that must be explored in God's Word. In our efforts to apply Scripture to our daily lives, we must understand that race is intimately tied to the American experience due to the turbulent relational history among whites, blacks, Native Americans, and other people groups in our nation. Race goes far beyond functioning as a designation of skin tone because certain pigmentation is affiliated with preconceived notions that society constructed, and these assumptions directly affect one's political, economic, and social experience. In short, race is a powerful factor that shapes our lives and influences our cultural context. In Southern Baptist life the opportunity to do theology from various contexts has been undercut. Formal theology has been disproportionately conducted by white men, and the context that their theology affirms has become standardized. This theological climate developed because our denominational press outlets, the most influential pulpits, and historically the majority of denominational executives have shared a single racial background and relatively few multicultural voices of equal influence have shaped SBC life.

Because Southern Baptists have normalized one particular context over others, matters that arise outside of that context tend to be dismissed as illegitimate. In fact, theological developments from nonwhite contexts tend to be deemed "proper" theology only when they engage issues that are pertinent to white culture and conform to "authorized" conclusions. This explains why issues like systemic injustice, racial oppression, economic inequality, and human rights that disproportionately affect nonwhite communities have remained largely unaddressed among Southern Baptists for so long. The reality of white cultural dominance among Southern Baptist theologians is consistent with what we already know to be true of all fallen humanity—we are self-interested creatures. Said differently, people (white and nonwhite alike) are interested in issues that are most pressing to them and are not as likely to contemplate deeply the circumstances of others.

In the current theological milieu, Southern Baptists from nonwhite backgrounds have three primary options when trying to integrate theology into their lives. First, they can deny their cultural identities in order to take on the approved dominant cultural norms, thus rendering them voiceless to their communities of origin. Second, they can choose the other extreme of rejecting the dominant culture and only identifying with their cultures, resulting in the continued marginalization of their voices. Third, they can bifurcate their theological work from the rest of their lives (theologizing like the first group) and respond to the pressing issues from their context without the accountability of their ecclesiastical and theological community. In the remainder of this chapter, I will explore a fourth path that brave minority trailblazers have traveled, namely, doing theology in community where multiple voices speak to the issues of the day. I hope that over time the fourth path will no longer be the exception but the rule.

Moving Forward

In large part the stain of racism in theology persists because little has been done to acknowledge that legitimate theology can emerge from majority and minority cultures alike. My hope is to affirm the theological curiosities of white and nonwhite believers and encourage theological development that allows believers faithfully to embody the mission of God in a way that is fitted to their context. In this final section I hope to recast the task of theology as leveraging the unity and diversity of the body in theological development. Revelation 7:10 depicts a chorus of voices from a multitude of racial backgrounds who cry out, "Salvation belongs to our God, who is seated on the throne." The single proclamation of the gathering depicts the unity of God's people around the person of Christ yet simultaneously testifies to his lordship over every tribe, tongue, and nation, whose voices contribute to the declaration. This biblical imagery, made possible by Christ's death and resurrection, literally produces a harmony that includes people of every culture. God's glory is made manifest in his ability simultaneously to inhabit and transcend the cultural uniqueness of each voice in the choir. This picture offers helpful hints for a theological model that can bleach the stain of racism from theology in the SBC. The elements necessary to apply this imagery to theological development are an understanding of the dialogical relationship among a person in context, Scripture, and the role of the church in the theological task.

Person in Context

The beauty of Revelation 7 is its witness to Christ's lordship over people from the corners of the earth. The Bible never indicates the bride will be monocultural because that would belittle God's glory and runs contrary to his mission. Any effort to escape human particularity by attempting to make one's own cultural context the standard is an effort to take on the role of God himself. Consequently, the beauty of this diverse chorus underscores the necessity of human particularity.

Every human is particular in that each person comes from a specific geographic location, socioeconomic status, upbringing, and racial background that together constitute his lived experience. In this social location a believer develops theology that guides his life to reflect God's redemptive mission in the world. In 1 Corinthians 13:12, the apostle Paul describes human limitation by contrasting the present age with the coming kingdom, saying we see "indistinctly, as in a mirror" or "in part," and we look forward to knowing ourselves, others, and our God "fully" in his kingdom. This means if a participant of the chorus imposes his part on the entire choir, the magnificent harmony of the gathering is reduced to a stale unison. A chorus of cultures united by mimicking a single cultural context, not centered on the gospel itself, falls short of the deep unity Christ purchased on the cross.

Scripture

Scripture, the chief source for guidance and wisdom, provides the unifying standard to which every believer appeals regardless of cultural context.

Although events and life situations that drive theological inquiry are often chronologically prior to an appeal to the Bible, Scripture is the ultimate authority to which contextual issues and Christians submit. Deference to Scripture results not only in knowledge, but in renewed faith and the ability to more effectively live as Christ in the world. Integrating Scripture into the Christian life involves interaction within the community of faith that enables believers to excavate the fullness of the Bible's significance in their contexts.

The Church

Christ's death and resurrection secured a foretaste of the kingdom, where believers can simultaneously embrace and together learn from the cultural differences that enrich the diverse tapestry of the body. As we anticipate the ability of seeing through a lens clearly in glory, undertaking theology in a diverse community of faith is God's provision for humans to see beyond their own limitations. In the spirit of iron sharpening iron (Prov 27:17), believers are able to benefit from one another's insights and perspectives as one new Spirit-filled humanity (Eph 2:14–15). Providentially, the most acute sharpening occurs along the lines of difference. In Southern Baptist life we have cherished the fruit of diversity with older Christians mentoring younger Christians (Titus 2:1–8) and in marriage as man and woman are satisfied when joined together. But Southern Baptists have largely neglected the opportunity of being sharpened across racial lines.

Superior theological development results from the diverse collective of the church (across ages, genders, races, and cultures) rather than from an individual or believers isolated in their cultural context. Spirit-filled voices from various walks of life help locate theological blind spots by identifying areas where a fellow believer's lived experience may have caused ignorance or apathy. Raising new questions that have origins outside a given context provides a cross-check that encourages faithfulness to God's restorative mission in the world. In order for cross-cultural collaboration to be fruitful, the SBC has to welcome minorities who cherish their cultures while primarily identifying with Christ. Only inviting people of color who deny their cultural heritage for acceptance in denominational life damages the cause of genuine biblical unity in our denomination. In essence, because our glasses are tinted differently, we can help one another see God's world more clearly together than we can apart, and in the process we will discover we have more in common than we ever anticipated.

I offer two areas of application for dominant-culture Christians. First, dominant-culture Christians need not feel condemned by this chapter and assume that their voices are no longer necessary or important. This chapter seeks to legitimize historically underrepresented voices in the theological exchange in order to blend them harmoniously with the long-standing pillars of Southern Baptist thought and life. Second, the influence of the dominant culture can be leveraged for the sake of liberating the voice of other believers so God's people can enjoy the fullness of equity and reconciliation in the body.

An implication of this model for historically marginalized groups is the imperative to understand the vitality of their voices. In essence, black and brown Southern Baptists must enter the theological conversation and be confident in their contribution, perhaps for the first time. Regaining a contextualized voice that will enhance the church's ability to achieve God's mission will, in all likelihood, be a slow process because the long-standing model has been for nonwhites to shed their cultural uniqueness and conform to the dominant culture. The challenge for historically marginalized voices is to begin projecting their theological voice without overcompensating for lost time or understandable frustration with the status quo.

Underrepresented voices are being invited to participate in mainstream denominational life like never before, but white and nonwhite Southern Baptists can still take proactive strides forward. The historically voiceless must be equipped to contribute to the theological dialogue at every level, from Sunday school classes and small groups, to the highest levels of seminary and university life. Minority voices can also create new spaces for healthy multiethnic theological engagement in cyberspace and by hosting conferences, seminars, and meetings to discuss topics relevant to the participants. In addition, teaching and preaching with biblical and theological rigor while capturing the best of a culture's traditions can help with removing the stain of racism from the SBC. Lastly, involvement in the seminaries and universities that house the thought leaders of our denomination and train an upcoming generation of Christians is a ready avenue for black and brown Southern Baptists to inject their new theological voices into denominational life.

Christ is Lord over all walks of life and speaks authoritatively into every cultural context. As his ambassadors, we are called to glorify him by embodying the imperatives of Scripture with the help and encouragement of the body of Christ. Some might ask, is removing the stain of racism from the SBC a theological issue? In the end the answer seems self-evident. But, in case it is not, let me say yes! This is a theological issue!

CHAPTER 5

The Role of Ethics in Removing the Stain of Racism from the Southern Baptist Convention

CRAIG MITCHELL

I n 1845, the Southern Baptist Convention (SBC) split from the Triennial Convention, which later became the Northern Baptist Convention (NBC), over the issue of slavery. Slavery was, at best, a complicated issue bound up in economic, class, race, and legal issues. Consequently, the SBC knew from the beginning that it had to do something about race. In 1845, the convention resolved "that the Board of Domestic Missions be instructed to take all prudent measures, for the religious instruction of our colored population."[1] This resolution affirms that black people are humans, made in the image of God, who need salvation in Jesus Christ and can benefit from gospel ministry. The resolution also implies the SBC struggled with the morality of racism even at its inception.

---

[1] For full resolution, see "Resolution on Colored Population," Southern Baptist Convention, accessed July 22, 2016, http://www.sbc.net/resolutions/31/resolution-on-colored-population.

Since the formation of the SBC in 1845, the denomination's leaders have passed thirty-one resolutions on race. Each one resulted from a growing realization that things were not right. For most of the SBC's existence, racism has been a reality within it. The issue of race and ethics in the SBC is one with many twists and turns, yet the convention has experienced a continual move to improve racial interaction.

Leaders

While others made contributions as well, three leaders stand out for their efforts in racial reconciliation. These are Thomas Buford Maston, Richard Land, and Foy Valentine. This section of the we describes these men and their roles in the changes the SBC has made in relation to race and ethics.

Thomas Buford Maston

With the ending of the Civil War and slavery, the SBC was slow to take strides toward racial reconciliation. For many years the SBC was located only in the South, and it held strongly to the racism endemic in that region. With few exceptions the SBC supported racism and Jim Crow laws. One of these exceptions was the professor of Christian ethics at Southwestern Baptist Theological Seminary (1922–1963), Thomas Buford Maston.

John W. Storey asserts, "While the exact origins of Maston's concern for racial justice cannot be pinpointed, his educational development no doubt broadened his understanding of social issues, including race."[2] After graduating from Carson Newman College in Jefferson City, Tennessee, in 1920, Maston continued his education at Southwestern Baptist Theological

---

[2] John W. Storey, "Thomas Buford Maston and the Growth of Social Christianity Among Texas Baptists," *East Texas Historical Journal*, vol. 19, no. 2, article 7 (1981), accessed July 22, 2016, http://scholarworks.sfasu.edu/ethj/vol19/iss2/7.

Seminary in Fort Worth, Texas. While working on his master's degree in religious education, Maston taught a course in applied Christianity. After completing his master's degree in 1923, Maston went on to receive his doctorate in religious education in 1925. He then pursued and earned a master's degree in sociology from Texas Christian University, which he completed in 1927. Afterwards, he entered Yale University, where he studied under H. Richard Niebuhr. He completed his PhD from Yale in 1939.

According to Storey, "Through two generations of students, many of whom have occupied important denominational positions, numerous books, countless articles in denominational papers, and the Christian Life Commission of Texas, Maston, more so than any other Texas Baptist, broadened the social awareness of his fellow Baptists."[3] Maston caused Christian ethics to be taught at all Southern Baptist seminaries. Many of his students fought against racism as well, which has contributed to the adoption of twenty-five SBC resolutions against racism since 1946. All of these efforts had good intentions, but they failed to deal with the central issues between the SBC and black Christians.

Maston was not content with thinking and talking about race, racism, and reconciliation. He was also directly involved in the fight for racial justice for black people. He even became a member of the NAACP. In 1959, he wrote *The Bible and Race and Segregation and Desegregation*. In addition to writing about issues of race in the SBC, he taught black men theology at night.

Richard Land

Richard Land is a native Houstonian and a sixth-generation Texan. His mother came from Boston, Massachusetts, and his father is a native of Houston. Within his family tree Richard Land has both abolitionists and slaveholders. With this unique set of family circumstances, Land gained

---

[3] Ibid., 31.

an important perspective that he has expressed throughout his life. He believes the people most liberated by the Civil Rights Movement were white Southerners. Land thought racism required white people to do things they knew were wrong. He also thought racism made white Southerners experience guilt that crippled their souls.

Land graduated *magna cum laude* with a bachelor of arts degree from Princeton University. As a part of his degree program, he wrote a 200-page thesis that explored the issue of slavery within the Baptist context. What he learned from this project further shaped his ideas on race relations. As he continued his education, Land gained a broader and deeper view of church history in general and Baptist history in particular. Further education included a master of theology degree from New Orleans Baptist Theological Seminary and a doctor of philosophy degree from Oxford University.

After finishing his education, Land taught as professor of theology and church history at Criswell College from 1975 to 1980. Land then served as Criswell College's vice president for academic affairs from 1980 to 1988. While on leave of absence from Criswell College, Land served from January 1987 to May 1988 as administrative assistant to Texas Governor William P. Clements Jr. Land was the governor's senior advisor on church-state issues and areas relating to "traditional family values" as well as antidrug, antipornography, and antiabortion legislation. In addition to these issues, Land had senior staff responsibility in the areas of public higher education, mental health, the physically handicapped, and AIDS.

Land is former president of the Ethics & Religious Liberty Commission (ERLC), the SBC entity assigned to address social, moral, and ethical concerns, with particular attention to their impact on American families and their faith. During his time in this office, Land worked with and fought for the rights of African-Americans in the SBC. When Land was hired as chief executive of the Christian Life Commission (CLC), the ERLC's precursor organization, he said during the interview process he would make racial reconciliation a major emphasis of his administration. Then as head of the CLC, he hired the first African-American to work in the SBC building in Nashville in a noncustodial role. When Southern Baptists apologized for their racist past in 1995, Land was a major factor in the process.

Foy Valentine

When Land took charge of the CLC, he began to address race and racism in the SBC and the need for reconciliation. To do so, he took the controversial step of inviting his predecessor Foy Valentine (1924–2006) to assist him in the effort. Valentine had led the CLC for thirty years and was on the other end of the theological and philosophical spectrum from Land.

Valentine grew up in the east Texas town of Edgewood in Van Zandt County. He earned an undergraduate degree at Baylor University in 1944, a master of divinity in 1947, and a doctorate at Southwestern Baptist Theological Seminary in 1949. At Southwestern he studied with Maston, whom he acknowledged as a key influence. In his doctoral dissertation, "A Historical Study of Southern Baptists and Race Relations, 1917–1947," Valentine wrote that he held out hope Southern Baptists would help to bring about the Christian way in race relations not by sponsoring legislative action or by fostering ecclesiastical fiats but by adopting, as individuals and as churches, the spirit and the mind of Christ in every phase of race relations. While a student at Southwestern, Valentine served as a special representative in race relations for the Baptist General Convention of Texas.

As a theological moderate in the SBC, Valentine opposed the conservative resurgence that took place within the convention during the 1980s–1990s. Nonetheless, Land welcomed Valentine's assistance in the work of racial reconciliation because it was one of the few issues on which they strongly agreed. Valentine's involvement was essential to bringing about the SBC's

1995 historic repentance of and apology for its involvement in all forms of racism, especially the racism committed against black people.

Valentine died in Dallas, Texas, on January 7, 2006. Land commented on January 11, 2006, at the funeral that "while Foy Valentine and I had significant differences of opinion on many issues, all Southern Baptists will be forever in his debt for his courageous and prophetic stance on racial reconciliation and racial equality in the turbulent middle third of the century." Land noted it had been important for him as a teenager in the 1960s to know Valentine and the CLC were on the right side of the race issue when too many institutions and individuals in American life and Southern Baptist life were on the wrong side.

Racial Reconciliation Consultation

As a result of the cooperation on race and racial reconciliation between Land and Valentine, the SBC eventually convened the Racial Reconciliation Consultation, January 16–17, 1989, at First Baptist Church in Nashville, Tennessee. Along with Land and Valentine, a number of other notables attended, including Jerry Sutton (pastor of Two Rivers Baptist Church in Nashville), Sid Smith (of the Sunday School Board—now known as LifeWay), Emmanuel McCall (director of the Black Church Relations Department of the Home Mission Board), and Lloyd Elder (president of the Sunday School Board).

The 1995 Resolution on Race

In 1995, the SBC celebrated its sesquicentennial in Atlanta, Georgia. In many ways this was a most appropriate time for the SBC to apologize for its role in slavery, racism, and the terrorizing of African-Americans. To ensure Southern Baptists addressed the issue of race at this historic convention, Land asked

SBC president Jim Henry to suspend the celebration until after the presenta-tion of a resolution on race. Land noted that many African-Americans who were working at the convention watched debate of the resolution with more than a little interest. When the vote was taken, some observers estimated 98 percent of messengers present were for the resolution.

Subsequent Resolutions on Race

In 1996, when the SBC annual meeting convened in New Orleans, Louisiana, messengers adopted a resolution on the arson of African-American churches. This resolution came about because at least thirty African-American church buildings were deliberately burned down in the 1990s. In 2007, when the SBC met in San Antonio, Texas, it adopted a resolution titled "On the 150th Anniversary of the Dred Scott Decision." After acknowledging the mistakes of the SBC, the resolution included the following:

> RESOLVED, That the messengers to the Southern Baptist Convention meeting in San Antonio, Texas, June 12–13, 2007, wholly lament and repudiate the Dred Scott Decision and fully embrace the Lord's command to love our neighbors as ourselves; and be it further

> RESOLVED, That we reaffirm the historic action in 1995 of the Southern Baptist Convention to "unwaveringly denounce racism, in all its forms, as deplorable sin," and to view "every human life as sacred . . . of equal and immeasurable worth, made in God's image, regardless of race or ethnicity"; and be it further

> RESOLVED, That we fully concur that "racism profoundly distorts our understanding of Christian morality"; and be it further

RESOLVED, That we commend our churches who intentionally reach out to all persons regardless of ethnicity, and we encourage all other Southern Baptist churches to emulate their example, as the Body of Christ is commanded and called to do; and be it finally

RESOLVED, That we pray for and eagerly await the day that the scourge and blight of racism is totally eradicated from the Body of Christ so that the world may see the love of Christ incarnated in and through us.

This resolution, like so many others before it, represents the desire of a denomination to do the right thing. In 2008, the first black president of the United States of America was elected. Consequently, the timing of this thirty-first resolution on race could not have been better. Along with President Obama's election came a resurgence of black liberation theology. The resolution states, "Racism profoundly distorts our understanding of Christian morality." Truer words are rarely spoken—not only for how white people relate to black people but for how black people relate to white people as well.

2012 to the Present

The election of Fred Luter as the first African-American president of the SBC in 2012 was a loud exclamation point on Southern Baptists' commitment to erasing the stain of racism from the convention. According to Danny Akin, president of Southeastern Baptist Theological Seminary, "The most significant event to happen in our SBC's history since our formation" is Luter's election.[4]

---

[4] Rick Jervis, "Pastor to Become First Black Leader of Southern Baptists," *USA Today*, June 7, 2012, accessed July 22, 2016, http://usatoday30.usatoday.com/news /religion/story/2012-06-11/fred-luter-to-lead-baptist-convention/55623616/1.

Amazingly, despite having a black president of the United States of America and a black president of the SBC, racial relations in America are at their worst since the 1960s (e.g., racial tensions from Ferguson to Cleveland). Moreover, although the SBC has made much progress since the 1950s, members need to do much more to erase the stain of racism from the denomination, such as supporting more nonwhite church plants. Significantly, in 2014, more than 58 percent of SBC church plants were nonwhite. In addition, the convention has seen notable increases in the number of black and brown individuals hired at seminaries and other SBC entities. To make sure this trend continues, at the annual convention meeting in 2015 (this time in Columbus, Ohio), those attending voted on yet another resolution, "On Racial Reconciliation." This resolution contains three important charges:

> RESOLVED, That we urge churches to demonstrate their heart for racial reconciliation by seeking to increase racial and ethnic diversity in church staff roles, leadership positions, and church membership; and be it further
>
> RESOLVED, That we urge Southern Baptist entities and Convention committees to make leadership appointments that reflect the racial and ethnic diversity of the body of Christ and of the Southern Baptist Convention; and be it further
>
> RESOLVED, That we continually prioritize and monitor our progress in adequately representing the increasing racial and ethnic diversity of our communities in our local congregations and our entities.

These statements encourage the SBC not to settle for the status quo but to keep trying to be racially inclusive at all levels, including leadership. To this end, an increasing number of ethnic minorities have been chosen for more places of leadership within the SBC. This is true in Southern Baptist churches, state convention leadership, and other places. Still, no minority has served as head of any SBC entity. To be sure, this is not an end unto itself, but one cannot help but believe someone from a minority group is qualified to lead LifeWay, the International Mission Board, the North American Mission Board, the Ethics & Religious Liberty Commission, GuideStone Financial Resources, the Executive Committee, or to serve as president of an SBC seminary. And minority SBC seminary professors are still a small group of men—so few that most of them are contributors to this volume.

Conclusion

Like every other sphere of this fallen world, the SBC is full of fallen people who are saved by the grace of God. While capable of great sin, they are given the grace to live supernaturally. Believers can forgive one another of wrongs done in the past. They can also move courageously into a future empowered by God's grace and mercy. What should be clear is that despite beginning with racist attitudes, the SBC has taken great efforts to move in the right direction. The struggle to maintain orthodoxy while holding onto orthopraxy is a difficult one. Nonetheless, just because something is difficult is not sufficient reason to quit. Instead, we should strive to achieve this goal. All races should work together and not lose heart in the attempt to build the kingdom of God. Galatians 6:9–10 admonishes us: "So we must not get tired of doing good, for we will reap at the proper time if we don't give up. Therefore, as we have opportunity, we must work for the good of all, especially for those who belong to the household of faith." May we labor together in love to remove the stain of racism from the SBC.

CHAPTER 6

"Play the Men": Preaching and Pastoral Steps Toward Removing the Stain of Racism from the Southern Baptist Convention

KEVIN L. SMITH

While heading into what appeared to be an overwhelming battle, the fighting men of Israel were told to "be of good courage, and let us play the men for our people, and . . . our God" (2 Sam 10:12 KJV). They were encouraged to fight like they believed God was on their side and to fight like they loved their people. Likewise, if the twisted historical mingling of Christianity and racism in American history is going to be removed, pulpits must be "manned" by courageous pastors that believe God's Word and love Christ's people.

In over two decades of preaching, I have seen the good, the bad, and the ugly as it regards the stain of racism among those that profess to be Christ followers—yes, the same Christ in whom "there is no Jew or Greek" (Gal 3:28). I have frequently praised God with much joy but also have called out to God in prayer with much disappointment. I have experienced rejection, by both black and white Christians, as I have sought to be a vessel of Christian unity among my tribe (Baptist folks, particularly the Southern Baptist Convention). Despite all, I think my burden is biblical, Christ honoring, and practically and pragmatically necessary in order for Christ's church to have a fruitful impact in America.

My Motivation

My desire to see the stain of racism removed from Christianity in America stems from the prayer of Jesus Christ as he headed toward his final act of love during his earthly ministry—his crucifixion. Certainly, I have the hope of ultimately praising the Lamb as part of a united and diverse assembly when we all get to heaven (Rev 7:9). Also, as part of my growth in godliness, I desire to obey the biblical command to make every effort to be unified in the Holy Spirit with other Christ followers (Eph 4:1–3). But the motivation that sustains me through the good, the bad, and the ugly is Jesus's prayer that his disciples would be united (John 17:21–23). Jesus Christ has laid down his life for sinners, of which I am one. I cannot read of his laboring in prayer concerning a Trinity-like unity among his disciples (yes, even the ones that formed a denomination in 1845 because of the issue of slavery) and be unmoved, wallowing in indifference or insensitivity. I cannot think of his costly sacrifice for me and choose the divisive idols of this society over him. I am continuously reminded by his Spirit that I cannot "serve two masters" (Matt 6:24 KJV), attempting to serve God and _____ (fill in the blank: racism, classism, sexism, ethnocentrism, etc.). Therefore, despite the hostile walls of division (Eph 2:14) that arise naturally in America, even among Christians, by the grace of the Holy Spirit, I intentionally and continuously reject those divisions and cling to the unifying Christ and his people—all of them.

My Christian (Baptist) Odyssey

In my childhood I attended a traditional black Baptist church affiliated with what was then called the American Baptist Convention (their black congregations were grouped as American Baptist Churches of the South). However, that church interacted broadly with churches from other black Baptist denominations and beyond. Thus, I was exposed to the four major black Baptist denominations, including black Methodists, black Pentecostals, and black congregations in largely white denominations (Episcopalian, Presbyterian, and Roman Catholic). I was born again under the ministry of a Methodist chaplain while attending Hampton University—a historically black college in Hampton, Virginia. I was ordained to the Christian ministry in the oldest Baptist association west of the Allegheny Mountains, the Elkhorn Baptist Association in Lexington, Kentucky. At that time I was a member of a historic black Baptist church that was dually aligned with the National Baptist Convention (NBC) and the Southern Baptist Convention (SBC). Former slaves had started the church in the 1850s.

Leaving Kentucky, I pursued theological education at the Church of God Theological Seminary in Cleveland, Tennessee. Interestingly, I was attending a largely white Pentecostal seminary, being supported by a scholarship from a mostly white Presbyterian foundation as I was planting a mostly black Southern Baptist congregation in an urban area under the auspices of the Tennessee Baptist Convention and the North American Mission Board. Our sponsor church was a mostly white Southern Baptist church in the suburbs. I pursued further theological study at The Southern Baptist Theological Seminary in Louisville, Kentucky, the flagship seminary of the SBC. After completing my doctoral classes, I was invited to serve as a member of the faculty, teaching in the areas of church history, preaching, and pastoral ministry. I spent nearly a decade serving as pastor of a traditional black Baptist church, leading that church into the SBC and affiliation with the Kentucky Baptist

Convention. Presently I serve as teaching pastor of a regional, mostly white, Southern Baptist megachurch. During my ministry I have served in a variety of roles in associational, state convention, and national SBC life. I have been invited to preach in many venues, SBC and beyond. In 2015, I was the first black man to be elected president of the Kentucky Baptist Convention. In each of my pastoral settings, I have emphasized biblical, text-driven preaching and teaching—which unavoidably leads to conviction and confrontation of sin. One such sin, which is undeniable in America, is racism.

"Play the Men" Against Racism

Preaching the Bible and leading Christ's followers is not work for cowards (Ezek 2:6; 2 Tim 1:7). Men who are scared, timid, or people pleasers will not be faithful in teaching and applying the truth of Scripture from the pulpit, especially when it involves correcting and rebuking (2 Tim 3:16). If the task of preaching is taken seriously, if the responsibility of pastoring Christ's disciples is weighed properly, then no sin can be tolerated or allowed to fester merely because the pastor is afraid or unwilling to deal with the scandal of confronting sin. Regarding the particular sin of racism, at least three considerations are relevant to preachers and pastors: their personal relationships, their understanding of leading from the pulpit, and their understanding of what repentance looks like in their particular ministry settings.

Personal Relationships

The pastor who seeks the credibility necessary to address such matters must demonstrate that racism and prejudice do not characterize his own life. Not only is this personal authenticity needed for credibility's sake; it is also required as that pastor examines himself as a disciple of Jesus Christ, making sure he is not preaching to others while playing the hypocrite. Do his friendships reflect any ethnic diversity? Have his children been exposed to ethnic diversity based on the guests that visit their home? What reaction, if any, do his kids observe in him when racialized conflicts occur in our society? What is his opinion of interracial marriage? These personal questions should be considered before the pastor seeks to address the sin of racism through his public leadership role. If he finds stains of racism in his personal life, then he needs to deal with those stains in order to provide Spirit-filled leadership as a pastor. The clear biblical response is repentance (1 John 1:9), followed by intentional efforts to develop relationships that reflect the rich glory of Christ's redeeming work, which creates a church composed of all kinds of people (Eph 4:3).

The personal relationships of a pastor are vital. They mark the difference between approaching Christian unity as a theory and approaching it as a matter of discipleship and seeking Christ's glory. Pastors have influence in at least two areas: their public preaching ministries and their leadership undergirded by the personal example of their lives. For example, when I was a church planter, the pastor of our sponsor church and I had a genuine friendship that spilled over into many interactions between our two congregations, such as men's retreats, women's prayer events, and youth trips. Now let me quickly note that genuine friendship is different from mere partnerships on paper, or paternalistic, condescending, patronizing interactions, or occasional impersonal pulpit swaps. The personal friendships of a pastor affect his life, his family, and the congregation he serves. Nothing confronts the stain of congregational racism like the obvious lack of such a stain in the life of its pastor.

The Pastor and the Pulpit

The pastor's pulpit ministry can contribute to removing the stain of racism from a congregation. His theology of preaching will impact how the task is approached. How do you understand the 2 Timothy 3:16 aspects of Scripture—teaching, correcting, training in righteousness, even rebuking? What does biblical application look like in light of your personality and the congregation's personality? Do you agree with historic Baptist confessions that the Scripture is our "rule for faith and practice" (i.e., sufficiency of Scripture)? Do you preach consecutively through large portions of the Bible, or do you select portions to preach based on a particular topic or doctrine you choose to address?

The Master Preacher, the Lord Jesus Christ, received differing responses to his various modes of teaching. His style of communication varied during his earthly ministry—speaking tenderly to the woman taken in adultery, speaking candidly to the woman at the well, verbally confronting religious hypocrites, and speaking provocatively on occasion. He did not lack clarity in his teaching. The common folk heard him gladly (Mark 12:37), and the religious leaders knew when he was rebuking them in his parables (Mark 12:12). Confronting sin in our preaching is challenging but necessary. Issues of fear, people pleasing, and popularity seeking, and will keep a pastor silent on sins like racism. Such hindrances to faithful pulpit leadership must be rejected!

Every human division that is used to separate people in sinful ways (racism, classism, sexism, ethnocentrism, etc.) must be confronted among Christ's people. Be prepared for your listeners to be defensive, dismissive, insensitive, indifferent, and sometimes angry. This is sometimes the reaction to the sanctifying rebuke of Scripture. One way to overcome these negative reactions is preaching that includes vivid application to assist your congregation in turning from the sinful patterns of thought and action that have characterized racial interaction in American history. As discussions of race and episodes of racial conflict arise in society, Christian congregations are not strengthened when their pulpits are silent in the midst of such confusion and darkness. Faithful preaching helps the saints see life, and think about life issues, through the lens of Scripture with a desire to bring glory to Jesus Christ and his gospel. Lack of application in preaching is less than faithful. No preacher should feel good if his congregation understands the sinfulness of racism yet has no idea how to repent and correct such matters in their personal and congregational lives. Prayerfully, sermons will feature Paul's term of application, "therefore" (Gal 6:10; Eph 4:1), as preachers give practical guidance to their listeners.

Occasionally I encounter a preacher who does not think the Bible addresses social issues like racism, and thus they should not be addressed from the pulpit. Nothing could be further from the truth! As it regards society at large, biblical teaching on the *Imago Dei* (Gen 1:27) and Jesus's command to "love your neighbor" (Matt 22:39) upends such claims. As it regards Christ's church, the prayer of Jesus (John 17), the command of Paul (Eph 4:1–3), and the picture in Revelation 5:9 should compel us to preach against the stain of racism. If a preacher practices consecutive exposition rather than topical sermons, issues of race, class, difference, kind, and "otherness" will naturally emerge in his preaching. Such preaching (we call it expository preaching) liberates the preacher in several ways. He is forced to preach the text instead of the current issues. Additionally, expository preaching helps the preacher avoid being accused of constantly talking about his hobbyhorse. Once more, expository preaching through biblical texts protects the preacher from focusing his preaching on current events and will protect him from being accused of targeting specific people or events in the congregation by focusing his sermons on them.

The Preacher's Life and Repentance

If a preacher's personal life does not bear the stain of racism and he believes the Scripture is sufficient to address this stain, he still must consider what the removal of the stain might look like in his particular ministry setting.

There is no one size fits all demonstration of repentance and righteousness in this matter. Questions abound. Must my congregation be multiethnic? Is it wrong to employ categories like "black church" and "white church"? Are we wrong if our church is all white, Latino/Hispanic, Asian, or black? Should Christians be "color-blind"? What if our church is located in a homogenous neighborhood? These are merely a sample of the relevant questions. Prescribing exact solutions for the myriad congregational settings, histories, and personalities is impossible. Let me suggest some issues for consideration as Southern Baptists push forward in our efforts toward removing the stain of racism from the SBC.

1. Patience. Many stains of racism are deep stains and will not be removed quickly or simply. Too often Christians want to cut the discussions short, avoid any disagreements, or seek quick-fix solutions. This is shortsighted thinking given the long history of racism within American Christianity.

2. Demographics. Some communities are homogenous while many others reflect a rich diversity of persons. In some communities multiethnicity is perhaps an unrealistic congregational goal. What should be considered sinful is a congregation's intentional refusal to engage its community because of racism/classism, which leads to indifference or insensitivity toward one's "neighbor."

3. Leadership/Authority. The role of a leader in various ethnic subgroups is surrounded by cultural dynamics. Therefore, as a church develops diverse leaders (staff, laity, group leaders, etc.), it must establish a leadership culture that recognizes the various cultural dynamics within that particular congregation. This is hard work!

4. Ethnicity/Culture. Even if a congregation rejects the sin of racism, many cultural issues related to diversity will still be challenges as the congregation "diligently [keeps] the unity of the Spirit with the peace that binds us" (Eph 4:3).

5. Immigrant Churches. In light of language challenges, assimilation obstacles, and other issues associated with immigration (especially first-generation immigrants), a melting pot country like the US will likely

continue to have a number of Christian congregations that provide an ethnic/cultural space for new arrivals.

6. "Black Churches." In light of American history, and the present-day tensions surrounding race in our country, "black churches" will likely continue for the foreseeable future. Should America have black churches? No, but that bridge was crossed in the early and mid-nineteenth century, due to white displacement of blacks in Presbyterianism, Methodism, and Baptist life.

7. Church Planting/Established Churches. The methodology for removing the stain of racism differs in church plants and established churches. Please consider the significant distinction involved in "building" a congregation without that stain versus transitioning a congregation that has been marked by that stain.

8. Music in Worship. If ethnically homogeneous churches have experienced worship wars, then one should not be surprised that this is a key issue in ethnically diverse congregations as well.

Conclusion

As pastor, seminary professor, and denominational leader, I pray that my many Southern Baptist brothers will preach the Word and live in obedience to the Word in their churches in such a way that the Spirit uses them to remove the stain of racism from the SBC.

CHAPTER 7

Administrative Steps Toward Removing the Stain of Racism from the Southern Baptist Convention

MARK A. CROSTON SR.

In 1988, Nike launched its trademark slogan, "Just do it." In the ten years that followed, Nike "increased its share of the North American domestic sport-shoe business from 18% to 43% (from $877 million to $9.2 billion in worldwide sales)."[1] Indeed, people continue to resonate with being positive, active, and aggressive when facing an issue. Just do it! When I was a student at The Southern Baptist Theological Seminary, Ernest White, who taught my leadership class, said leadership is the "moving on" ministry, management is the "eyes on" ministry, and administration is the "hands on" ministry.

Our theme for this book, and for this chapter, centers on the phrase "the stain of racism." What I know about stains is that we have to work hard to remove them. I have never had a stained article of clothing and decided I

---

[1] "Mini-case Study: Nike's 'Just Do It' Advertising Campaign,'" CFAR, UDOC, accessed July 22, 2016, https://time2morph.files.wordpress.com/2012/09/nike_just-do-it1.pdf.

would just set it aside, believing the stain would disappear or that somehow the stain would naturally get better with time. In fact, the contrary is often true. Stains left alone only get more set and stubborn. When humankind was lost and stained with sin, God did something about it. In love, he sent his Son, Jesus, to shed his blood on a cross. Ephesians 5:27 states, "He did this to present the church to Himself in splendor, without spot or wrinkle or anything like that, but holy and blameless."

At the administrative level Southern Baptists must keep working relentlessly to remove the stain of racism from the Southern Baptist Convention (SBC). James 4:17 says, "So it is a sin for the person who knows to do what is good and doesn't do it." In the rest of this chapter, I offer administrative steps Southern Baptists must take if we want to remove the stain of racism from our convention.

1. Do not submit to fear of man. As a pastor for thirty years and a preacher for thirty-five, I know ministry is difficult if fear of losing one's job serves as the motivation for doing ministry. Pastors and denominational leaders know, at times, to expect repercussions, even among the faithful, of standing for Jesus. We tend to rationalize to ourselves that it is alright to give in to what we know is wrong because we must live to fight another day.

Judge Paul Pressler stated in his book *A Hill on Which to Die*:

> In any great movement are individuals who sit back and watch to see which way the battle will go. When they see which side will prevail, they attach themselves to that side. These people disturb me, because they seem to be self-serving individuals who are more interested in their own advancement than they are in basic principles. They are more concerned with their own future than they are with the cause itself.[2]

---

[2] Paul Pressler, *A Hill on Which to Die: One Southern Baptist's Journey* (Nashville: B&H, 2002), 297. Excerpt accessed July 22, 2016, http://www.baptistbanner.org /Subarchive_5/500%20Excerpt%20Hiil%20on%20which%20to%20die.htm.

Pressler went on in a Baptist Press article to say, "The heroes of the conservative movement are not those whose names were in the press. They were the grassroots people who loved the Lord and loved the convention and loved God's Word and wanted to make sure that Southern Baptists returned to what [the Bible] teaches."[3] Removing the stain of racism requires this kind of commitment.

2. Step forward. Steps can always be taken by those who are willing to take them. Ecclesiastes 9:10 says, "Whatever your hands find to do, do with all your strength." Juana Bordas, author of the book *Salsa, Soul, and Spirit: Leadership for a Multicultural Age*,[4] shares eight ways to practice multicultural leadership:

- Get a history lesson.
- Think *we*, not *I*.
- Practice generosity, not greed.
- Flatten the leadership structure.
- Help people learn how to work together.
- Create a sense of "family."
- Foster a culture that's accepting of spirituality.
- Focus employees on a company vision.

Southern Baptists might benefit from these practical steps if they intentionally incorporate them into the leadership structures of our Southern Baptist organizations.

3. Hire diverse leaders. Southern Baptists should take a lesson from the business world. Business leaders know that if they want to reach a diverse community, then that community needs to see ethnic representation in their

---

[3] Jeffrey Robinson, "Pressler: Conservative Resurgence Was Grassroots Movement," Baptist Press, March 30, 2004, accessed July 22, 2016, http://www.bpnews.net /17956/pressler-conservative-resurgence-was-grassroots-movement.

[4] Juana Bordas, *Salsa, Soul, and Spirit: Leadership or a Multicultural Age*, 2nd ed. (San Francisco: Berrett-Koehler, 2007).

company's leadership. The August 2015 issue of *Ebony* magazine contains an article titled "The Diversity Divide."[5] Playing off the term "digital divide," it looks at several of the leading technology companies and their workforces. Seeing those companies whose workforce resembled the diversity of the society in which we live was refreshing. When we look at our SBC entities, the ethnic demographic of their leadership matches neither society in general nor the diverse membership of Southern Baptist churches. Hiring people just like us is easy. Yet SBC entities must hire more qualified black and brown people to serve in leadership, and the SBC must put more black and brown people in positions of leadership and influence if in fact the convention wants to remove the stain of racism from its midst.

4. Be partners rather than patriarchs. When people try to build relationships, the recipients of those overtures often know whether the initiators are authentic or patronizing. On far too many occasions, those with leadership and influence in organizations handpick leaders from minority groups who more closely reflect the culture and values of the white majority than of the diverse black and brown people they are called to serve. If the chosen leaders do not have a track record of leadership in the minority group, the minority group will have difficulty identifying with them as leaders. They are seen merely as puppets put in place by paternalistic majority leaders.

Patriarchs make decisions and inform the minority constituents. Partners get to sit at the table, cook the food, eat the food, and lead in the dinner table discussions. They give perspective and insight, and their voices are heard before decisions are made.

5. Persevere. Did I say this was not going to be easy? When I was the new senior pastor at my first church twenty-eight years ago, I excitedly told

---

[5] For the full story see, "Diversity Divide," *Ebony*, July 24, 2015, accessed July 22, 2016, http://www.ebony.com/photos/career-finance/diversity-divide#axzz 48KRdEaV0.

my mother of the many things I thought needed to happen to get the church moving in the right direction. My saintly, wise, old mother told me, "Son, remember, it's not the speedboat of Zion. It's the old ship of Zion." I knew exactly what she meant. A speedboat can turn on a dime as you whiz here and there. The old ship of Zion does not turn so fast. The captain gives the order to turn to the helmsman. The helmsman makes the turn on the bridge. The rudder in the stern of the vessel turns immediately with the helmsman. Yet the old ship keeps going in the same direction. It takes a while before the action of the rudder in the ocean changes the momentum of the ship and begins to move it in a new direction. In my pastorate some things at the church changed right away. However, some things took many years to change. But praise God they changed. Through that experience I became convinced of this: since God appointed me as that particular church's pastor, if I stood there at the helm long enough preaching his Word, then one day those things would change.

Both the SBC and the stain of racism are old. Read the history chapter again if you forgot. Remember that at every point of progress, a brave person stood up by the power of the Spirit and said, "Some things are going to change around here." And for doing this, some paid a price. Southern Baptists serious about removing the stain of racism from the SBC must recognize this stain will not be erased without a hard, painful, and long fight. But we must not (indeed we cannot!) give up this fight. We must go the second mile. Give the extra effort. Be faithful over a few things. Persevere and watch God work.

6. Untie the convention from political parties. Political party affiliations are not inherently bad. But when a convention whose task is to reach the world with the gospel begins to impose or advocate a political agenda as part of its mission, this is bad. If we merely align with a party, whenever the party does something wrong, the SBC gets painted with a broad brush. We have to find other ways to stand on our biblical morals and convictions

concerning specific issues. We should support specific candidates but not fully align with any political party platform. God and the gospel cannot be limited to the whims of a political party. The Republicans are not always right, and the Democrats are not always wrong. And the opposite is also true! You cannot eat at the king's table and still declare like Nathan, "Thou art the man" (2 Sam 12:7 KJV). Ours is to be a prophetic voice, not merely a political one.

As an example, to be passionate about the unborn is right, but it comes across as disingenuous if we are not also passionate about the living who are poor and oppressed. James 1:27 says, "Pure and undefiled religion before our God and Father is this: to look after orphans and widows in their distress and to keep oneself unstained by the world." This is one of those areas that causes distrust and at times makes the stain deeper.

7. Love. One thing I have always appreciated and admired about the SBC is our wholehearted and unfaltering commitment to missions and evangelism. This has been our heartbeat from our beginning in 1845 until now. The fight that got us started was over sending more missionaries to the field. We put our money where our mouth is in support of missions and evangelism, but if we are going to remove the stain of racism, we must elevate the Great Commandment to the same level as the Great Commission. We love Matthew 28:19–20: "Go, therefore, and make disciples of all nations, baptizing them in the name of the Father and of the Son and of the Holy Spirit, teaching them to observe everything I have commanded you. And remember, I am with you always, to the end of the age." But we must also live by Matthew 22:37–40: "Love the Lord your God with all your heart, with all your soul, and with all your mind. This is the greatest and most important command. The second is like it: Love your neighbor as yourself. All the Law and the Prophets depend on these two commands."

Conclusion

"By this all people will know that you are my disciples, if you have love for one another," Jesus says in John 13:35. The apostle Peter writes, "Now the end of all things is near; therefore, be serious and disciplined for prayer. Above all, maintain an intense love for each other, since love covers a multitude of sins" (1 Pet 4:7–8). Southern Baptists love to pray for revival. Our prayers for revival must include prayers for reconciliation in our denomination. However, prayer is not enough! We must pray and act. If when we rise from our knees God gives us hearts to love all races in our denomination, then we will see revival.

CHAPTER 8

Educational Steps Toward Removing the Stain of Racism from the Southern Baptist Convention

KEVIN M. JONES SR.

Introduction

Racism and education are inextricably linked. As W. E. B. Du Bois argued in *The Souls of Black Folk*, his prolific study of race relations, the problem of the twentieth century was the problem of the color line. I believe this problem extends to the twenty-first century as well and to the classroom in particular. Du Bois stated, "But when we have vaguely said that Education will set this tangle straight, what have we uttered but a truism?"[1] Even so, every entity, each church, and the entire Southern Baptist Convention (SBC) should consider how to advance racial reconciliation by means of education.

When I lead my family in morning devotions, I have the unique freedom to worship God in a way many of my African-American ancestors could not. The Lord commanded the people of Israel to teach his commandments

---

[1] W. E. B. Du Bois, *The Souls of Black Folk* (New York: Bantam Classic, 1903).

diligently to their children (Deut 6:4–9). But one cannot teach what one does not know. And sad to say, the institution of slavery, along with subsequent Jim Crow laws, robbed generations of African-Americans of having the option to know God through rigorous theological education. Indeed, many slaves were forbidden from learning to read, and the separate black and white schools that dominated public education for most of the twentieth century were anything but equal, depriving black children in some cases of basic grammar, vocabulary, and reading skills. Obviously this hindered African-Americans in their study of the Bible. Because of racism, a key segment of Christ's body in America was inhibited from obeying fully the command to learn God's commands and teach them diligently to their children. To the contrary, I have an entirely different experience on a daily basis when I open up the Bible and teach it to my family. Thus, in my view, education in Southern Baptist life can play a vital role in helping to remove the stain of racism from the SBC.

Jawanza Kunjufu, in his book *Critical Issues in Educating African American Youth*, borrows from a paradigm developed by Barbara Sizemore. Kunjufu states:

> You first establish what the problems are, then you ask yourself what caused the problems, and lastly, you determine the implementation of those solutions. We seem to spend a lot more time in the first stage, the problem stage, which reminds me a great deal of what happens when the media glorifies the negative, but rarely looks at: (1) what caused the problem, (2) what are some of the solutions to the problem, (3) the implementation of those solutions.[2]

R. Albert Mohler Jr., Matthew J. Hall, and Jarvis J. Williams address causes of racism within the SBC. Other contributors to this volume offer possible

---

[2] Jawanza Kunjufu, *Critical Issues in Educating African American Youth* (Chicago: African American Images, 1989).

solutions. Take heart, be encouraged, and begin implementing those recommendations. In the remainder of this chapter, I offer simple suggestions to help remove the stain of racism from the SBC.

1. Cooperate in Education

In *Conceiving the Christian College*, Duane Litfin suggests ways to improve Christian colleges:

> How can Christian colleges attract and retain an excellent student body? How do we recruit and then facilitate the work of a first-rate faculty? How do we keep pace with the ever-quickening demands of technological change, much less harness these changes to enhance our student's learning? How do we keep our cost low enough, and our student aid high enough to remain accessible to a wide variety of students, all the while funding strong academic programs? How are we to diversify our campus communities, drawing in more of those minority populations who have not traditionally been attracted to Christian Colleges?[3]

A cursory glance at many seminaries reveals they are doing well addressing challenges raised by the first three questions. Yet many of those same seminaries, especially Southern Baptist seminaries, often have failed to recruit and retain minorities.

There is some truth to the statement, "Where there is a will, there is a way." If there is a genuine desire for SBC seminaries and Baptist colleges and universities to address Litfin's fourth challenge, then Southern Baptists likely will find a way. An important component of the way forward is cooperation among churches from different ethnic postures that have the will

---

[3] Duane Litfin, *Conceiving the Christian College* (Grand Rapids: Eerdmans, 2004), 3.

and specific proposals for increasing attendance of minorities at Baptist institutions of higher education. To clarify, this does not mean every Southern Baptist (white or black) will be equally equipped or passionate to carry out the educational task of removing the stain of racism from the SBC. But no one person can carry out this task alone. The stain of racism is too dark for that. If Southern Baptist churches cooperate cross-racially to enhance ethnic minorities' access to education, then we can make the stain less apparent. "Where there is a will, there is a way."

2. Read Books by Black and Brown (Non-Anglo) Authors

Intellectual racism, though often unintentional, is prevalent in the SBC. Reading and encouraging others to read books by and about non-Anglos is one way to help remove the stain of racism from the convention. Some readers may prefer to strategize their reading in categories: e.g., theology, biblical studies, church life, history, cultural studies, and literature. My college professors and mentors have always provided me with diverse selections of literature. Before Tom Schreiner, Tom Nettles, Hershael York, and Greg Wills were my colleagues, Kevin L. Smith and Curtis A. Woods provided me with their books and articles, and they read them with me. They also challenged me to put what I learned into practice and monitored my progress. Regarding diverse reading, Albert Mohler says, "Read all the titles written by some authors. Choose carefully here, but identify some authors whose books demand your attention. Read all they have written and watch their minds at work and their thought in development. No author can complete his thoughts in one book, no matter how large."[4] Take note of the

---

[4] Albert Mohler, "Some Thoughts on the Reading of Books," September 25, 2015, accessed October 10, 2015, http://www.albertmohler.com/2015/09/25/some-thoughts-on-the-reading-of-books-3.

authors in the suggested reading in Appendix 1 of this volume. Consider Mohler's strategies.

All of the books I read shape me regardless of whether the author is white or black or brown. However, books written by or about African-Americans shape me in a different way since I share similar cultural experiences with the authors or characters in those books. For example, a book that shaped me focused on *Teaching Adolescent Males to Read: Closing the Achievement Gap.*[5] In that book Alfred Tatum gives insight into the task of educating struggling minority males. As a part of a strategy for teaching these young men, he challenges the reader to give them books written by African-Americans. This book grants much insight about minority adolescents that likely would be unavailable in a book about majority adolescents. Books shape our minds. Movement starts in the mind with a thought. Dallas Willard states in *Renovation of the Heart: Putting on the Character of Christ,* "As we first turned away from God in our thoughts, so it is in our thoughts that the first movements toward the renovation of the heart occur. Thoughts are the place where we can and must begin to change."[6]

The preceding point is so important that I want to develop it further. I am suggesting that you read non-Anglo authors on a regular basis, not just during Black History Month. Southern Baptists in a broad array of occupations and cultural settings must diversify their reading lists. In fact, I suggest that if Southern Baptists want to see the stain of racism removed from seminary to the pew, then the entire denomination must critically and seriously consider a widespread curriculum change that includes more vetted writers/ authors, professors, pastors, and leaders from ethnic groups that have been traditionally marginalized. I am speaking of cultural enlightenment and a paradigm shift. This sort of curriculum development might be difficult in

---

[5] Alfred Tatum, *Teaching Adolescent Males to Read: Closing the Achievement Gap* (Portland: Stenhouse Publishing, 2005).

[6] Dallas Willard, *Renovation of the Heart: Putting on the Character of Christ* (Carol Stream: NavPress, 2014), 95, Kindle.

certain contexts. But Southern Baptist homeschoolers and private schools have more freedom to make the academic curriculum as rigorous and as ethnically inclusive as the leaders in those contexts would like.

Even those who are not formally involved in education can read books and recommend them to others. Everyone is a teacher, like it or not. Someone at some point will ask your opinion about something. Therefore, we all should strive to learn something new and fresh each day. Consider reading non-Anglo authors as morning reading, right-before-lunch reading, immediately-following-lunch reading, right-before-the kids-complete-school reading, or simply go-to-bed reading. Beverly Tatum states, "If young people are exposed to images of African-American academic achievement in their early years, they won't have to define school achievement as something for Whites only. They will know that there is a long history of Black intellectual achievement."[7] Be encouraged. You can influence change in this way whether you are white, black, or brown. You can help remove the stain of racism from the SBC by means of education.

A great example of what I am explaining comes from one of my white colleagues at Boyce College. Bryan Payne, associate professor of Christian theology and expository preaching, and I often have conversations about race and reconciliation. He reads books with and to his kids about and by African-Americans. With great humility he often says to me, "We have so much to learn." I would guess that many men and women are like Brian. This example leads me to my next practical guide.

3. Become Aware of African-American Scholars

As I stated above, as an undergraduate student at Kentucky State University, I read many books by African-American scholars. Although often ignored or

---

[7] Beverly D. Tatum, *Why Are All the Black Kids Sitting Together in the Cafeteria? and Other Conversations About Race* (New York : Basic Books, 1997), 65.

dismissed by mainstream white scholarship, many African-Americans complete research and contribute to theological, sociological, political, and educational advancements. Their writings are broad, deep, and speak to more than issues affecting minorities. One way to familiarize yourself with minority scholarship and literature is by subscribing to a journal that African-Americans produce and edit.[8]

4. Reform Seminary Curriculum

One can tell what an academic institution values by looking at the curriculum. A quick look at the curriculum at The Southern Baptist Theological Seminary demonstrates our strong commitment to biblical languages and theology. As a result, we attract many students who want to focus on these areas. Theological institutions have an opportunity to remove the stain of racism by revising course requirements to include marginalized voices. Racial reconciliation requires mutual understanding. As Albert Tate states, "I have to know white culture by default. I can't get a GED without having to understand white culture. But a white person can get a Ph.D. and never know black culture."[9]

It might be difficult, but it is possible for every seminary to have every student take an African-American history class, or at the very least incorporate into existing courses (e.g., Baptist history, church history, Cooperative Program course) the role and impact of non-Anglos in the history of the Christian movement. I am not suggesting an elective. An elective might wrongly suggest to some that the subject is not vital or significant. These

---

[8] See, for example, *The Journal on Negro Education, The Journal of African American Studies, The Journal of Black Studies, Callaloo: A Journal of African Diaspora Arts and Letters,* or *The Du Bois Review: Social Science Research on Race.*

[9] John Richards, "'A Time to Speak' Panel Recap, Reformed African American Network, December 16, 2014," accessed November 10, 2015, https://www.raa network.org/time-to-speak-recap.

courses should be required. To reshape the landscape and mind of the seminary student, curriculum reform at some level should happen sooner rather than later. We see this happening in numerous areas (e.g., missions, evangelism). Why can't we reform the curriculum in such a way that it equips future pastors and theological educators with the intellectual goods to minister in an increasingly racially diverse world?

I recognize that accreditation agencies have a thing or two to say about curriculum. Like it or not, each accredited institution marches at some level to the drumbeat of its accrediting agency. But here is a simple proposal: Students should be required at SBC seminaries, as well as Baptist colleges and universities, to earn multiple hours of credit in courses centered on the impact of non-Anglos on the Christian movement. Curriculum modification will expose students to thousands of pages written by African-Americans and other non-Anglos and will afford them multiple conversation partners. Seminaries should find professors qualified to teach these courses. An African-American identity is not required to teach an African-American history class successfully. However, diligent research and attention to racial difference are both necessary.

5. Professors, Supplement Your Courses with Additional Readings and Lectures

As one of my colleagues at Southern Seminary says, the professor is the curriculum. Of course, this statement needs to be appropriately nuanced and clarified. But its central idea is correct: the professor determines what the curriculum will be and how she or he personally fits within it. As many professors know, curriculum changes at our SBC seminaries take time. However, additional literature and lecturers can be inserted in a course immediately. One of my colleagues, Jarvis J. Williams, gives at least one lecture on the importance of reading black and brown authors each semester in almost every class he teaches at the seminary, including New Testament, Greek exegesis, hermeneutics, introduction to Second Temple Judaism, and doctoral-level courses on Second Temple Judaism and Pauline soteriology. In my courses I regularly do the same. If I do not expose my students to non-Anglo authors, chances are they won't be exposed to them in my field.

Professors should use the syllabus, class lectures, visiting professors, and multimedia to introduce their students to non-Anglo literature, history, music, and culture. This is in addition to core course requirements. I do not assume this will give students a full picture of, for example, the diverse African-American experience. But I am convinced this is a good place to start.

Some SBC founders viewed African-Americans as less talented as or of less value than whites. Professor, use your influence over the syllabus to help rectify this false and sinful perspective. If professors do not create their own syllabi, they can still incorporate suggested reading. A professor with a terminal degree should have the ability to find and implement quality non-Anglo scholarship in her or his classes.

6. Form Reading Groups

The Commonweal Project is an initiative at The Southern Baptist Theological Seminary to equip Christians in general and pastors in particular with a biblical theology of work and economics.[10] Through this initiative I have participated in multiple reading groups with other faculty. In short, we select books, read them, and discuss implications and implementation of them over lunch. I lead students in the same types of discussions, often using books by authors from marginalized groups. I choose a book, then generate interest, select students who are interested in reading the book, and have conversations about

---

[10] "About Us," The Community Project, accessed November 19, 2015, http://www.thecommonwealproject.com/about-us.html.

topics addressed in the book. Professors can use this as an opportunity to read books written by African-American and other minority authors.

7. Read Non-Anglo Authors as Part of Pastoral Apprentice Programs

I referred earlier to Kevin L. Smith's efforts to introduce me to many authors. While he served as my pastor, he did the same thing with other young men in our church who were called to ministry. He led us in reading works like *Introducing Christian Doctrine*[11] by Millard J. Erickson, which strengthened my understanding of God. As my pastor, Smith provided me with systematic engagement around pastoral issues. One way pastors can mentor future ministers is by exposing them to a variety of authors from different ethnic postures in addition to Anglo. Expertise surrounding these authors is not a requirement but only a humble willingness to learn with and from them. After I completed my own pastoral apprentice program, I was delighted when the elders of the church were open to adjusting the material of the apprenticeship to spend concentrated time teaching African-American history.

8. Lead Within Your Organization

Maybe you feel unequipped to lead or do not see yourself as a leader within your organization. Maybe you are unsure of how to make changes where you are employed or volunteer. Fear not! Many biblical figures such as Moses, Joshua, Nehemiah, and Gideon were imperfect leaders. Yet God was with them. The God of the Old Testament is the God of today. Leading does mean you have to work with every member of your organization. Engaging one person is leading.

---

[11] Millard J. Erickson, *Introducing Christian Doctrine* (Grand Rapids: Baker Academics, 2001).

Professor, author, and activist Cornel West says, "We need leaders—neither saints nor sparkling television personalities—who can situate themselves within a larger historical narrative of this country and our world, who can grasp the complex dynamics of our peoplehood and imagine a future grounded in the best of our past, yet who are attuned to the frightening obstacles that now perplex us."[12] You have the capacity to transform an organization. Identify an area of weakness in your own understanding of African-American or some other aspect of non-Anglo history. Next, assess what resources are available for you. Purchase some if necessary. Then establish a realistic action plan for your own professional development as a leader. Evaluate your progress and make needed adjustments. Ask coworkers in your church or ministry to join you in a journey of learning to appreciate the educational contributions of all men and women made in the image of God.

9. Fund Scholarships for Minority Students

The following sentences are not about reparations but ministry to brothers and sisters in Christ in light of the financial, spiritual, emotional, and physical pain caused by racism. I suggest Southern Baptist churches donate to Baptist colleges and seminaries, beyond their giving through the Cooperative Program, for the purpose of establishing foundations and scholarships to assist qualified minority students with financial needs in their pursuits of theological education. Each institution could create a leadership team with diverse members to discern how to allocate these funds to worthy recipients. Some institutions within and outside the SBC have already established teams and scholarships and provide proof of increase in minority enrollment.

I understand that academic institutions function as businesses. They must educate and turn a profit. Nonetheless, Baptist colleges, universities, and seminaries can help black and brown students without privilege and

---

[12] Cornel West, *Race Matters* (Boston: Beacon Press, 1993), 7.

access (and I am fully aware that many have both) get a quality education. I know firsthand that SBC institutions of higher learning want to increase minority enrollment. One way to do this is to provide, when and if possible, financial help. When students (black or white) have excellent experiences at a seminary, they will likely in turn share that with their churches. Church members might, in turn, be willing to reciprocate support of the seminary through increased Cooperative Program or designated scholarship funds.

Let this illustration envisage my point. A new store just opened in a mall a few miles from my house. In order to draw new customers, the store gave away thousands of dollars' worth of clothes. In return, they have new customers in my wife, all of her friends, and many others. My wife was amazed at many items behind the door—items she saw because she went to the store. SBC seminaries are great training grounds for ministry. However, not enough minorities are behind the doors to come out of the seminaries and tell others about their experience.

A large number of African-Americans, especially those from traditional African-American churches, are skeptical about SBC seminaries. One reason is that they perceive racial injustice and inequality in the SBC. If SBC seminaries can financially assist in the education of African-Americans and other ethnic minorities, this could help change their perspective. To be clear, I am not requesting a welfare program for minority students. Instead, I am suggesting that SBC academic institutions should be willing and eager to help academically qualified and vetted minorities with scholarships if the institutions are able.

10. Use Oral History

I stated previously that one should read books by African-Americans and other non-Anglos or those books centered on their experiences. But education requires us both to read books and listen to lived experiences of all types of people. Harvard psychologist Howard Gardener's Theory of Multiple

Intelligences offers clear evidence of multiple learning paths. Some learn linguistically and musically. Therefore, listening to music, poetry, and other forms of auditory art by minority artists can assist some students in understanding diverse ethnic experiences.

Historically, African-Americans have been an oral people. The emphasis on orality in African-American life and culture is not accidental. On the contrary, it was a system set up by Anglo-Americans to assure African-Americans were not taught to read or write. Consider, for example, the case of Frederick Douglass. As a slave, Douglass was intrigued with reading because his master's wife would often read the Bible aloud. (Yes, the book that clearly explains all humans were made in the image of God was being read to a boy enslaved for having dark skin. Embrace the irony of that scene.) Douglass wanted to read the Bible aloud himself, so he quickly learned the alphabet and short words. He was a skilled reader in a short while. However, he discovered that reading was not for slaves. His master's wife was scolded for teaching him to read and instructed to stop. Douglass recalled the interaction in his autobiography:

> He forbade her to give me any further instruction, telling her in
> the first place that to do so was unlawful, as it was also unsafe;
> "for," said he, "if you give a nigger an inch he will take an ell.
> Learning will spoil the best nigger in the world. If he learns to
> read the Bible, it will forever unfit him to be a slave. He should
> know nothing but the will of his master, and learn to obey it.
> As to himself, learning will do him no good, but a great deal of
> harm, making him disconsolate and unhappy. . . . She finally
> became even more violent in her opposition to my learning
> to read than was Mr. Auld himself. Nothing now appeared to
> make her more angry than seeing me, seated in some nook or
> corner, quietly reading a book or newspaper. She would rush
> at me with the utmost fury, and snatch the book or paper from
> my hand, with something of the wrath and consternation which
> a traitor might be supposed to feel on being discovered in a

plot by some dangerous spy. The conviction once thoroughly established in her mind, that education and slavery were incompatible with each other, I was most narrowly watched in all my movements.[13]

11. Embrace Mutual Sacrifice

Paul in 1 Corinthians 9:19–23 writes:

> For though I am free from all, I have made myself a servant to all, that I might win more of them. To the Jews I became as a Jew, in order to win Jews. To those under the law I became as one under the law (though not being myself under the law) that I might win those under the law. To those outside the law I became as one outside the law (not being outside the law of God but under the law of Christ) that I might win those outside the law. To the weak I became weak, that I might win the weak. I have become all things to all people, that by all means I might save some. I do it all for the sake of the gospel, that I may share with them in its blessings. (ESV)

Paul was in bondage to no one but submitted himself to all. He was employed by no man but made himself available for all. He conducted himself as a servant to all. Paul became all things to serve all people. Paul labored. Paul acted as if he had no privileges. Paul did anything necessary to reach people. We also should seek to become like the ones we wish to reach in order to win them to Christ. This will require sacrifice, commitment, and humility. In Acts 16:3 ESV, "Paul wanted Timothy to accompany him, and he took him and circumcised him because of the Jews who were in those places, for they all knew that his father was a Greek." Paul understood Timothy needed to

---

[13] Fredrick Douglass, *The Most Complete Collection of Written Works & Speeches*, (New York: Northpointe Classics, 2011), Kindle Electronic Edition 1317–21.

make a sacrifice in order to serve. Jews would have been offended if Timothy was not circumcised. So Paul circumcised Timothy. The point is this: removing the stain of racism from the SBC via education requires all the different races within the convention to make sacrifices—especially our white brothers and sisters.

Conclusion

One cannot ignore Barbara Henry's bold acts. In 1960 she was the white teacher of first-grader Ruby Bridges, the first African-American student to integrate into her school in Louisiana. Henry taught Bridges one-on-one for an entire year. Each day the two had to make their way past angry mobs while protected by federal marshals. Henry was bold. In the face of a dark and bleak situation, she did not cower but did her part. Like Henry we all have a part to play in education, not just the pastors. May God help all races of Southern Baptists work to remove the stain of racism from the SBC by making a relentless commitment to the kind of education that tells the whole truth and nothing but the truth.

CHAPTER 9

Publishing for Church Leaders to Remove the Stain of Racism from the Southern Baptist Convention

TOBY JENNINGS

A Brief History of Education

Conquerors and rulers of ancient civilizations were well aware of the power of at least two tools of cultural formation: education and assimilation of a populace. To be sure, megalomaniacal rulers perverted education into mere indoctrination, but all understood that knowledge is power. Ancient Persia, for example, acquired the appellation "the cradle of civilization" for its cunning empire-wide implementation of institutions and policies that not only sustained unity within the empire, which is purported to have ruled approximately 44 percent of the earth's population at its peak, but were so consequential that many of those innovations still permeate cultures around the world to this day.[1]

---

[1] Ehsan Yarshater, *Enclyclopaedia Iranica* (London: Routledge & Kegan Paul, 1996), 47. See also, Guinness World Records, "Largest Empire, by Percentage of World Population," in *Guinness Book of World Records*, accessed July 23, 2016, http://www.guinnessworldrecords.com/world-records/largest-empire-by-percentage -of-world-population.

Greek prince Alexander the Great, who eventually defeated Persia, set about to Hellenize the known world. Because he recognized the power of assimilated knowledge, he determined to indoctrinate his empire with Greek language and culture as he had learned as a pupil in Aristotle's academy. In order for such a prodigious undertaking to take effect, the emperor's edicts would have to be published abroad, whether by delivered scroll or word of mouth.

Fast-forward a couple of millennia to a different political construct and early era of American education where "the three Rs—reading, writing, and arithmetic" were fancied as the foundation for learning. Leaders of the new republic recognized that the power of literacy is liberty. Regardless of socioeconomic or ethnic heritage, these foundational loci of learning were sufficient to equip learners to explore the world around them with their God-given capacity as his image bearers and to assimilate knowledge for both personal and community flourishing as well as the advance of human culture as commanded and granted by God in the cultural mandate of Genesis 1:26–28. Reading, writing, and arithmetic could allow learners to drink richly from the well of their forebears and become the repositories of knowledge for their own posterity, thereby fulfilling God's creative purpose for humanity to image our Creator in near limitless ways from generation to generation.

Print Media Publishing

All who instruct must first have learned. While the chief modes of learning prior to the advent of the printing press were necessarily more communal and interpersonal (e.g., storying, oratory, recitation), the advent and prolif-eration of print media facilitated as many distinct opportunities for learning as there are imaginative individuals with access to these media. One can see, therefore, how publishing quickly attained pride of place among vehicles of instruction. Further, the medium continues to adapt to keep pace with advances in media technology.

Publishing is an invaluable tool for dissemination of knowledge. Any endeavor to employ publishing equitably and honorably, therefore—whether to educate, entertain, or inspire—should follow the divine directive of Micah 6:8 to do so with justice, kindness, and humility before the God who published the singular greatest message ever communicated. Consideration of ethnicity is at best secondary in this endeavor. That is not to say, however, that cultural or linguistic distinctives are wholly insignificant. Contextualization is as key for understanding original meaning as it is for communicating contemporary import.

Consider, for example, the centuries-long Western practice of portraying biblical Jewish figures, including Jesus, as Anglo-European. Commendable medieval artistic expression notwithstanding, such inaccurate portrayals of God's human self-disclosure—well intentioned as they may be—can produce unintended effects, not the least of which is imaging humanity's Messiah in a way he never intended to disclose himself.[2] Some of these effects then become engrained in society, trumping the cultural preferences of divine revelation. To grasp the gravity of such an error, one need only read in Exodus 32 the account of the reimaging of God by his own covenant people and the consequences visited upon them for portraying him as they thought most appropriate at the time.

Philosophically, arguments have been made that a publisher's inventory should reflect its audience statistically. For example, if a market consists of 65 percent Anglo-American, 18 percent Latino-American, 10 percent African-American, and 7 percent Asian-American, then the imagery, illustrations, colloquialisms, etc., in the organization's inventory should reflect precisely those statistics. Vision and prudence, however, may suggest an alternative strategy, depending on an organization's mission. For example, if a publisher

---

[2] In Deut 4:1–24, for example, God delivers to Israel, which had no direct experience with the incarnation, an intentional imperative to receive and believe him through the hearing of his inspired Word—his *torah*—rather than any man-imagined form; see also Rom 10:9–17.

intends to broaden and diversify both its customer base and global impact, the statistical majority of its base may not elicit the investment of resources or attention a minority segment does. Moreover, if the statistical majority is motivated to diversify, then targeting that majority may in fact have a reverse effect—not to mention the potential of being contrary to the mission of Christ to pursue with intentionality "people for God . . . from every tribe and language and people and nation" (Rev 5:9; see also 7:9). Christian publishing may well, then, intentionally reflect diversity more than homogeneity, particularly in light of the desired goal.

Ethnocentric Publishing Houses

While the majority of American publishing houses may not legitimately be said to have as their focus intentionally marketing and selling to America's majority ethnic population (which, by the way, will no longer exist as a majority by 2050, according to the U.S. Census Bureau),[3] a few publishing houses and divisions are directed by a strategic vision to reach particular ethnic or cultural groups. Certainly instructional benefits are realized from cultural contextualization, the challenging question of what constitutes legitimate contextualization notwithstanding. A detriment, however, could be the unwitting perpetuation of ethnocentrism or an air of disunity within the universal body of Christ as well as a pathos contrary to Christ's own mission to break down dividing walls among his single flock (Eph 2:13–18; John 10:16).

Unity in diversity is not merely an ancient Greek philosophical construct. As many early Christian thinkers asserted, all truth is God's truth.[4]

---

[3] Jennifer M. Ortman and Christine E. Guarneri, *United States Population Projections: 2000 to 2050* (Washington, DC: U.S. Census Bureau, 2014), 4, accessed July 23, 2016, https://www.census.gov/population/projections/files/analytical-document09.pdf.

[4] Augustine said, "Nay, but let every good and true Christian understand that wherever truth may be found, it belongs to his Master; and while he recognizes

God is the one who envisioned, designed, and implemented both his diverse creation and his plan to restore it to its original beauty and unity. The gospel inherently entails reconciliation. So-called gospel publishing that neglects illustrating this unity in diversity may well not qualify as "good news" publishing, for it publishes only mediocre news.

So what is a solution? Americans are skilled at casting vision, undertaking endeavors, and seeing them through to completion. Following humanly unsystematized movements of the Holy Spirit is more challenging, however, because doing so requires faith. How might we discern how the Spirit of God is directing his church in the matter of diversification and lead in accord with such a reviving movement?

Enigmatic Revival

In his book *Revival and Revivalism*, Iain Murray notes that a chief attribute among some of history's great awakenings was the proliferation of public discourse about God and his redeeming activity.[5] In light of John's vision of Christ's bride in Revelation 5:9 and 7:9, one might argue that the stirrings of revival are upon our own generation. Not only have recent surveys shown a reconfiguration of Western Christendom, but conversations about racial unity and diversity are abounding, whether compelled by nationally

---

and acknowledges the truth, even in their religious literature, let him reject the figments of superstition, and let him grieve over and avoid men who, 'when they knew God, glorified him not as God, neither were thankful; but became vain in their imaginations, and their foolish heart was darkened. Professing themselves to be wise, they became fools, and changed the glory of the incorruptible God into an image made like to corruptible man, and to birds, and four-footed beasts, and creeping things' (Rom 1:21–23)." Augustine, *On Christian Doctrine* (Pickerington: Beloved Publishing, 2014), 58.

[5] Iain Murray, *Revival and Revivalism: The Making and Marring of American Evangelicalism 1750–1858* (Carlisle: Banner of Truth, 1994).

publicized tensions or the Holy Spirit's impressing and equipping specific public figures to be more articulate about the matter, or both.

Evangelical publishers certainly may lead in heralding the vision given to John. If revival is beginning to occur, no precept mandates that it will manifest identically to awakenings in the past. Nor does any precept suggest God's church (and her publishing "weaponry") is forbidden from being proactive in attentiveness to what the Holy Spirit is communicating (like the sons of Issachar; see 1 Chr 12:32) and publishing this good news broadly (Luke 4:14). Gospel publishing should posture itself as always reforming, listening to the Holy Spirit as he speaks through circumstances as well as his diverse people, learning from history and our brothers and sisters of all stripes, and leading with a message in concert with the choir in Revelation 7:9 "from every nation, tribe, people, and language . . . standing before the throne and before the Lamb."[6]

---

[6] This listening, learning, and leading posture was articulated by Thomas Rainer, president and CEO of LifeWay Christian Resources, to messengers of the Southern Baptist Convention's 2015 meeting in Columbus, Ohio. Rainer communicated that the Nashville publisher recognizes and endeavors to engage "the kingdom of God and its great ethnic diversity." Rainer affirmed LifeWay's cultural engagement philosophy with three emphases "to make certain that our organization . . . is truly reflecting of the kingdom of God." (1) Listen. Being predominantly Anglo-American in its staffing and customer base, LifeWay has endeavored recently to host and listen to other ethnic groups within its customer base. The intent is to give audience to customers and their cultural distinctives in order to provide the most effective discipleship resources to service a diverse (and diversifying) customer base. (2) Learn. LifeWay's vision is to provide "biblical solutions for life." In order to best provide such solutions to a diversifying customer base, LifeWay intends to continue to listen to and learn from precisely those customers. In attestation to the organization's intentionality, Rainer affirmed that LifeWay currently offers more than 1,000 resources in a non-English language including thirty-five different languages. (3) Lead. "Quite frankly," warned Rainer, "if the leadership of an organization is not leading in this endeavor to reflect the diversity that is in the kingdom of God, it won't happen." Rainer's full presentation may be viewed at http://live.sbc.net.s3-website-us-east-1.amazonaws.com/ondemand .html [shortened link: http://bit.ly/1G0KSVJ].

Conclusion

May God use our publishing agencies within the SBC to help us continue to work relentlessly to remove the stain of racism by the materials we publish for all of our churches!

CHAPTER 10

Are We There Yet? Concluding Thoughts About Removing the Stain of Racism from the Southern Baptist Convention

CURTIS A. WOODS

I f you have ever traveled a long distance with small children, I am certain you have heard the question, "Are we there yet?" Typically, most parents or caregivers answer the first inquiry with a lowered voice and soothing demeanor—"No honey, we have not arrived." After the tenth query, however, parents often allow the backseat inquisition to evoke a different response. In a split second they retort: "Be quiet. Be patient. Don't ask me that question again." Once the executive order has been issued in the parliamentary confines of the vehicle, a deadly silence between parent and child settles over the car.

Race relations in the Southern Baptist Convention (SBC) cannot commence on the level of parent-child interactions. When family members cry foul, exposing inconsistencies within our denominational history, every friend of the gospel should listen humbly and respectfully regardless of ethnic or racial identity. An unwillingness to listen and learn from one another will only produce denominational paternalism. The SBC's dialogue on race, racism, and reconciliation should be different from the parent-child dialogue, for we are brothers and sisters in Christ. As such, every ethnic tribe within the SBC must pursue unity in the midst of diversity.

No one person in our convention has all the answers on eradicating racism in the SBC. But we do have some answers. We are yokefellows and sojourners, looking for the blessed hope, the appearing of our great God and Savior, Christ Jesus (Titus 2:13). Without an eschatological hope, conversations about how systemic racism plagues our convention and country will end in nihilism. We are prone to hopelessness without the liberating power of the gospel. Our hope is built on nothing less than Jesus's blood and righteousness. Christ Jesus is our hope. And our hope in Christ is certain since hope is based on a person (1 Tim 1:1; Heb 6:18–20).

The contours of racialization are observed on virtually every epistemological canvas in America. Each contributor to this volume wrote candidly about his lived experience. Some are more poised and less affected by the historic stain of racism in the SBC. This is apparent by the tone of their criticisms. Others, shall I say, seem to release years of pent-up frustration and pain caused by the stain of racism in the SBC. Both postures deserve a sympathetic hearing. Conversations about racism in the SBC are never easy. No one wants to be called a racist. And yet the reality is that we all have resonating within our hearts hints of racism because of our fallenness and, in some cases, because of our upbringing.

Since the question of race relations in Southern Baptist history is so complex, the editors wisely solicited professors, administrators, and practitioners to discuss and offer some biblical, theological, and practical solutions to the stain of racism in the SBC. This work is a composite of church history, systematic theology, biblical theology, practical theology, and educational leadership. I thoroughly enjoyed listening to the collective wisdom of each writer— especially since, as a member of the Kentucky Baptist Convention's executive staff, I serve 2,400 ethnically and geographically diverse churches across the commonwealth. I know many of our churches want to remove this dreadful stain but often lack the appropriate tools to do so. Many of these churches are not insolent or indifferent toward race matters, just ill informed. Perhaps this work will aid their efforts to advance the good and pursue kingdom diversity for the glory of God. Before I go further in this chapter, I think readers should know my story as it relates to race, racism, and reconciliation in the SBC.

One Man's Sojourn

In 2006, I left a ministry in Dallas, Texas, at Oak Cliff Bible Fellowship to become the campus minister at Kentucky State University in Frankfort, Kentucky, a historically black institution. I was unaware I would become the only African-American male working full-time for the Kentucky Baptist Convention (KBC), the largest Protestant denomination in the state. To my knowledge, the only time the convention actively pursued hiring an African-American male in a full-time capacity was to serve the Baptist Campus Ministry at Kentucky State. Also a part-time position, created years prior to my hiring, in cooperative ministries was held by Lincoln Bingham, a faithful African-American pastor who spent years working toward reconciliation. In 1976, the KBC established the Department of Interracial Cooperation and hired Bingham to bridge the relational chasm between African-American and Anglo-American Baptists in Kentucky. Matthew J. Hall's chapter notes the social divide created when Anglo-American Baptists lost legal power over their African-American Christian brothers and sisters.[1] There was a

---

[1] Matthew J. Hall, "Historical Causes of the Stain of Racism in the Southern Baptist Convention." Hall states, "For their part, black Baptists quickly developed their own formalized networks of churches. While the SBC included roughly 650,000 churches before the war, their numbers declined significantly after the conflict when emancipated slaves rushed out of their former churches to begin their own new churches and association."

great exodus of African-Americans from predominantly Anglo-American denominations.[2]

At the time of my hiring, we had three full-time African-American staff members. I was the only African-American male along with two African-American females. One served in a clerical role while the other, who recently earned a doctorate from Southern Seminary, led our women and seniors ministry. I remember how much angst I felt when I observed the dearth of African-Americans involved in full-time denominational ministry in Kentucky. In light of the lack of color, I automatically assumed tokenism. It seemed the convention needed to house an African-American campus minister at the commonwealth's only historically black college or university. The lot fell on me.

In my frustration I revisited a provocative *Time* magazine article published in 1962 by Martin Luther King Jr. entitled "The Case Against Tokenism."[3] I could hardly believe King's critiques easily fit my situation well over four decades later. I cannot stomach tokenism within any organization. Employees never achieve full buy-in once tokenism is discerned. Nevertheless, I remained faithful to my campus-ministry role while positioning myself to pursue doctoral studies on the implications of American racialization on the Christian mind in general and the African-American mind in particular.

On July 2, 2012, I assumed the role of associate executive director for the KBC. I am one of few African-American males, to my knowledge, serving in an executive leadership position within any Baptist state convention in cooperation with the SBC. In light of my appointment, the world can no longer adjudicate SBC state executive leadership, *whites only*. As such, I was intrigued by Mark Croston's chapter on administrative steps toward

---

[2] Ibid.

[3] See Martin Luther King Jr., "The Case Against 'Tokenism,'" *The New York Times*, August 5, 1962, accessed December 30, 2015, http://www.thekingcenter.org /archive/document/new-york-times-case-against-tokenism#.

removing the stain of racism. I resonated with two of his suggestions to ameliorate our current racial dilemma: "hire diverse leaders" and "be partners rather than patriarchs."

As a denominational leader, I can only speak for the KBC. In Kentucky, Paul H. Chitwood, KBC executive director-treasurer, has made significant strides to diversify our mission board staff. In fact, recruiting competent and cooperating hires is one of my top leadership priorities alongside our state executive. We live or die by the men and women we bring on our missional team.

Shortly after my appointment, the evangelism and church planting team leader brought three candidates to the table to serve in full-time roles. In line with our hiring vision, we searched for men who were the best fits for the jobs based on evangelistic passion, not ethnic persuasion. We found men who affirmed our mission, values, and core distinctives in word and deed. And, to my delight, each hire was an ethnic minority.

The first hire was an African-American leader who became my successor at Kentucky State. The other two recruits were Hispanic leaders hired to support our church planting strategist. Since our current church planting strategist is Hispanic, we are arguably the only state convention that has three Hispanic men providing overall leadership to church planting efforts. Or, put another way, they are not simply ministering to Hispanics!

Prior to Chitwood's election the convention employed bifurcated church-planting strategies. An Anglo served predominantly Caucasian churches, and a Hispanic strategist worked with nonwhite churches. When state conventions intentionally demarcate ministry along racial lines like this, we institute a form of ecclesiastical Jim Crowism insofar as there are two ministerial doors one may enter to receive help. One door figuratively reads "whites only" and the other "ethnics." In fact, I cringe each time I hear an SBC leader use the term "ethnics" to reference nonwhites only. Such usage is sociologically misguided and etymologically shortsighted. Every image bearer is ethnic. And, therefore, when *ethnic* becomes the universal descriptor for nonwhites, we unwittingly subjugate and marginalize every person of color. They become, in no uncertain terms, "other." No matter how much someone from the majority group smiles when she or he says "ethnics," the term screams privileged class—author, designer, chief.

Moreover, oftentimes when persons of color are hired to lead within the SBC in any capacity, their roles directly relate to particular ethnic groups as opposed to all people groups within convention life. This hiring practice tacitly says people of color are only qualified to work with their own kind. Of course, when organizational changes are made without any feedback from persons of color in the boardroom, position descriptions often fit the pale of constituent members who conceive jobs in echo chambers. A chorus of different voices around the table is needed to quell monophonic and monoethnic ideas.

As such, our KBC mission board makes sure people of color have authoritative seats around the table. In fact, we can boast of having an Asian-American and African-Americans serving on our administrative committee beside men and women from diverse geographic regions of the commonwealth. Our administrative committee vets and recommends all staff hires to the mission board. To quote our executive director, "They are our bosses." Hence, to say these men and women have the most important role in convention life would be an understatement. There are no rubber stamps. Every hire must go through the evaluation fire. We all know our tendency to hire persons who remind us of ourselves, so the mission board intentionally mitigates potential discrimination by having diverse voices at the vocational planning stage. We are not in favor of cronyism in our KBC.

In order to attract more persons of color to our convention, we have eradicated the racialized idea that each ethnic group should serve its own little constituency. In other words, we are not selective. When a Kentucky Baptist church calls for help, we do not first ask, "Is this an African-American, Caucasian, Hispanic/Latino, or Asian church?" Our staff has already decided to help any church, at any time, in any location according to our giftedness. Thus, I should be as comfortable preaching to friends in the mountains of eastern Kentucky as I am ministering in urban west Louisville. We lovingly take the gospel to the hills and to the hood without fear of ethnic or geographic differences. Our trust is in the power of the gospel to change hearts and strengthen Christ's bride.

R. Albert Mohler Jr. is correct to say, "Our confidence is not in our ability to extricate ourselves from the stain of racism." Only God has the power to cleanse our racist spots. Yet we must do the hard work of sharing leadership and influence in the SBC in order to erase the stain of racism from the convention. People of color who are called to serve within SBC life often evaluate reconciliation based on the majority culture's desire to release leadership and influence. When SBC leaders refuse to relinquish leadership and influence, they invariably enforce the perception of placation in the corridors of marginalized hearts. Perhaps the greatest act of faith within our convention will be when SBC entities hire nonwhites to give primary leadership to our convention.

An Abundance of Counselors

"Where there is no guidance a nation falls, but there is success in the abundance of [wise] counselors" (Prov 11:14 NET), says the sage. I approached reading this work like a student before transitioning to the role of counselor. I learned so many wonderful things from the contributors. Although the majority of the contributors are African-American, Kevin Jones and Jarvis J. Williams invited three significant white SBC voices to provide historical perspectives and personal reflections from their perches of influence. I will interact with their ideas before conversing with selected counselors due to space limitations.

R. Albert Mohler opened the work with a courageous chapter that high-lights our sin and God's glorious grace. He answers the question of how an SBC conceived in sin could also be called by the gospel to expand the kingdom worldwide. Mohler invokes Psalm 51:5 to lay the foundation for his treatise on removing the stain of racism. David, after being confronted by Nathan, declared, "Behold, I was brought forth in iniquity, and in sin did my mother conceive me" (ESV). In straightforward prose Mohler explains how citizens in the North and South imbibed racist beliefs. For Mohler, no one in the American political economy receives a pass from what Frantz Fanon called the "white gaze"[4] of ethnocentrism, not even the venerable Abraham Lincoln or the founders of The Southern Baptist Theological Seminary. He states, "White superiority was claimed as a belief by both Abraham Lincoln and Jefferson Davis, but the Confederacy made racial superiority a central purpose. . . . Further, notable Southern Baptists James P. Boyce and John Broadus were chaplains in the Confederate Army." In context, Mohler essen-tially declares that the founders of Southern Seminary were racists. Now, as an African-American Southern Baptist, hearing the ninth president of one of the world's most influential evangelical seminaries declare this truth warmed my soul. He spoke the truth in love and seemed not to be concerned about losing supporters. Mohler exemplified Kevin Smith's admonition that racial reconcilers cannot be "scared, timid, or people pleasers" in applying the truth of Scripture if they desire true change.[5]

Mohler avoids revisionist history by speaking prophetically against our ugly but usable past. In so doing, he says, "We cannot change the past, but we must learn from it. We have no way to confront the dead with their heresies, but neither do we have any way to avoid the reckoning we must make and the

---

[4] Frantz Fanon, *Black Skin, White Masks*, trans. Richard Philcox (New York: Grover Press, 1952).

[5] Kevin L. Smith, "'Play the Men': Preaching and Pastoral Steps Toward Removing the Stain of Racism."

repentance that must be our own."[6] Repentance is the key that unlocks the door to reconciliation. And real repentance is patient with others when the same question is asked again and again. Perhaps this is why Mohler asserts, "Our commitment to Christ requires that we confess in every generation the sin in which this convention was conceived and the sin that remains."[7]

Matthew J. Hall offers principles for true reconciliation based on historical truth telling in line with Mohler's sentiments, by saying, "But for us, as a convention of churches, ever to see true gospel reconciliation within our fellowship, a measure *of historical truth-telling* [emphasis added] is required, a stance that is not always comfortable, popular, or simple."[8] Hall rightly believes the way forward is committing to speak the truth in love. "Truth cuts falsehood to pieces," wrote Dietrich Bonhoeffer.[9] We cannot experience reconciliation when unity is based on a lie. When historians, or any Southern Baptist, tell the Southern Baptist story from a hagiographical slant, it pours salt on an easily opened, racialized wound. That is to say, SBC officials who euphemize historical white supremacy in America unwittingly stymie racial reconciliation efforts in our convention.

Daniel L. Akin is one of the leading SBC seminary presidents when it comes to race relations and recruitment. Akin pursues kingdom diversity by recruiting, training, and supporting myriad students of color on master's and doctoral levels at Southeastern Baptist Theological Seminary in Wake Forest, North Carolina. According to Akin, kingdom diversity is enmeshed in the school's DNA. Akin has seemingly raised the bar for every Baptist higher learning institution by modeling racial reconciliation in the form of financial

---

[6] R. Albert Mohler, "Conceived in Sin, Called by the Gospel: The Root of the Stain of Racism in the Southern Baptist Convention."

[7] Ibid.

[8] For more information on pursuing truth-telling in historiography, see Joyce Appleby, Lynn Hunt, Margaret Jacob, *Telling the Truth About History* (New York: W. W. Norton, 1994).

[9] Dietrich Bonhoeffer, *Life Together* (New York: Harper & Row, 1954).

aid for qualified students. If our convention desires stronger churches that reflect a kingdom mosaic, erasing the stain of racism, we must allocate funds to attract students who would otherwise gravitate toward culturally familiar theological training institutions.

Akin delivers a penetrating nail to racism's coffin, saying, "Overcoming racism requires of the majority race humility and sacrifice, virtues that do not come easily." Once again an SBC leader acknowledges places of privilege held by Caucasians in the convention without denigrating family members of any ethnic group. Humility, according to Akin, is necessary because few people give up privilege and power without a fight. In the past the racial war was overt, but in twenty-first-century denominational life the privileged walk is often covert until exposed by those in authority.[10] Akin rightly acknowledges how easy it is to invite someone into a community without making any real sacrifices to make them feel welcome. He goes on to say Southern Baptists' newfound family members should receive an "invitation to the table of leadership" and, after proper vetting, a call to "sit at the head of the table."

K. Marshall Williams Sr. is the voice crying out in the wilderness of Philadelphia. Like many other contributors Williams contends white supremacist ideologies and racist misinterpretations of Scripture soiled the SBC. He prophetically calls for repentance and renewal for the sake of the gospel and the Lord's church.

I appreciate Williams's candor. But I would add to his sharp rebuke that many white brothers and sisters fought for and with African-Americans in the cause of racial reconciliation in the SBC. Just read, for example, Craig Mitchell's essay. More to the point, although many white racists used the heretical curse of Ham theory to justify racial hierarchy within the SBC, other white Southern Baptists argued against it. In 1956, Robert Lane Hughes,

---

[10] For more information on overcoming white privilege through understanding the privilege walk, I recommend an essay by Peggy McIntosh entitled "Unpacking the Invisible Knapsack." A pdf is readily available via a basic Internet search.

according to T. B. Maston, wrote an unpublished doctoral dissertation on the meaning of ארור in Genesis 9:18–27.[11] In it, explains Maston, Hughes debunks the exegetically flawed notion that Noah's curse affected all Hamites as opposed to the descendants of Canaan.[12] Maston also sets a flame to the devilish curse of Ham in his chapter entitled "Cursed Be Canaan."[13] Thus, although some within the SBC perhaps have not repented of the curse of Ham theory, others have. We must fight for historical balance as we critique friends, family, and foes. Craig Mitchell offers the kind of balance I think is necessary on this matter. I, for one, was unaware of the numerous race resolutions made throughout our convention's history. According to Mitchell, the thirty-one resolutions on race suggest Southern Baptists have grappled with the so-called "Negro problem."[14] Perhaps some knew their ungodly dealings with fellow Christians of different hues would bring forth a reckoning.

In terms of biblical theology, Jarvis J. Williams and Walter Strickland lay Scripture and evangelical theology bare when they analyze the meanings of race and biblical community. Williams holds the distinction of being the only African-American New Testament scholar in SBC life. He writes and speaks consistently on race and theology in multiple venues. Williams's chapter incorporates history, sociology, critical race theory, and New Testament scholarship into a candid conversation about the myth of modern racial reasoning.[15] He also shows how Bible interpreters err when they read modern views of race into ancient texts. Williams counsels readers to delineate how the ancients used racial categories over and against contemporary

---

[11] T. B. Maston, *The Bible and Race: A Careful Examination of Biblical Teachings on Human Relations* (Nashville: Broadman, 1959), 114.

[12] Ibid.

[13] Ibid.

[14] See Craig Mitchell's essay, "The Role of Ethics in Removing the Stain of Racism from the Southern Baptist Convention."

[15] For more information on the myth of modern racial reasoning from a theological perspective, see J. Cameron Carter, *Race: A Theological Account* (New York: Oxford University Press, 2008).

understandings. According to Williams, the ancients lacked pseudoscientific, presuppositional biases contemporary thinkers bring to the fore when discussing race.[16]

Strickland treats the stain of racism with a theological cleanser. He clarifies what happens when one group of people or one particular context postures itself through a normalizing framework. Strickland explains, "By normalizing one particular context over another, matters that arise outside of that context tend to be dismissed as illegitimate." Strickland's counsel resembles Peter Berger's concept of a plausibility structure, which I explain below. Strickland keeps the universality of sin and the noetic effects of fall foremost. He argues that "sin makes us self-interested and protective creatures. Sin makes issues affecting our communities the apex of social problems." Strickland's counsel is clear. Social ills find their genesis in sin, and these ills are eradicated by faith in the coming King. In order for the SBC to remove the stain of racism, Baptists must celebrate the eschatological vision given to the beloved through the bodily resurrection of Christ. Strickland proclaims the gospel by saying, "Christ's resurrection secured a foretaste of the kingdom where believers can simultaneously embrace and together learn from the cultural differences that enrich the diverse tapestry of the body." We are better together.

Mitchell, mentioned above, honors the legacy of countercultural heroes, including Maston and his *protégés*. Mitchell acknowledges these

---

[16] I'm befuddled that Williams, the only African-American New Testament scholar teaching at any Southern Baptist college or seminary (to my knowledge) and the only four-time graduate of the flagship Southern Baptist Theological Seminary, is virtually never given invitations to address Southern Baptists on a national level or to speak at Baptist colleges, universities, or seminaries on matters related to his expertise—in spite of the fact that he has published books on the intersection of soteriology and race, peer-reviewed academic articles/essays on Pauline theology, and a plethora of popular articles on the intersection of gospel and race for various media outlets. Could this too be because of the role racism plays in power dynamics within the SBC?

courageous men and women who fought for racial equality at the risk of death. We should honor the few Southern Baptist pastors, denominational leaders, scholars, and laypeople alike who were on the right side of the civil rights tracks lest we propagate the myth that Southern Baptists as a whole did not care about racial reconciliation and the gross injustices historically committed against black and brown people. Some were indifferent to race matters, and others were insolent toward freedom fighters, but some Southern Baptist leaders were fortresses of courage and ministers of reconciliation.

These leaders attacked the paternalistic strain of Anglo-American hegemony in the culture at large and in the SBC. Many of these servants were ostracized by their SBC kin. And yet they continued to beat the drum of justice. In the words of Maston, "While we should have no particular desire to be martyrs, we should not forget that as long as our society and people in general fall below God's standards, there is something wrong if all men speak well of us."[17] Beautiful! Not every SBC leader missed the social justice train. Some cried, "All aboard."

His Heart Is Black

Several years ago I read a provocative book on SBC race relations entitled *His Heart Is Black*. I happened upon the book laying patiently on a "free books" table at Georgetown College in Georgetown, Kentucky. Frankly I had walked by the table hundreds of times without any desire to read its smorgasbord of questionable titles. However, this time was different. I felt a nudge almost beckoning me to *take up and read* the tattered gray book, bearing ripped pages coupled with what seemed to be water or coffee stains on the front and back portions. If I judged the book by its cover, I would have tossed it aside without a second glance. So why did I go the extra mile?

---

[17] Maston, *The Bible and Race*, 49.

The answer was the phrase, *His Heart Is Black*. Like any cultural colloquialism, those who have been initiated will hear certain words or phrases with caution or commendation. Certain African-Americans use this expression as a term of endearment for Anglo-Americans who aided emancipatory efforts for African peoples from the first days of slavery until now.

While reading page after page, I was cut to the quick. I was overwhelmed by joy when I discovered narratives of six men who stood against overt racism when racial reconciliation in Southern Baptist churches was arguably an elusive dream. Interestingly enough, most of these men did not share my soteriological convictions or, even, hermeneutical approach. Yet we march to the same reconciliation drum. My contribution to this volume questions the theory of ubiquitous hatred in every quarter of the SBC. We must acknowledge all who bore the Southern Baptist moniker from 1845 till now. Some were liberals, some moderates, and some conservatives. They all have a chapter in the racial reconciliation story.

As a Southern Baptist leader of African descent, I honor the sacrifices made by men who understood and protected the personhood of those who share my descent against the aggressive tide of southern racism. Can you imagine derision from your own denominational kin because you rightly rejected and corrected racialized hermeneutical ideas even though you were shouted down by the majority? Well, many African-American Christians experienced repudiation for centuries when they confronted evil systems of race-based supremacy. Like African-American Christians of yesteryear, SBC leaders who spoke prophetically against falsehood became social pariahs and ecclesiastical vagabonds.

Amending the Rules

Guy Bellamy, who in the opinion of some was an apostle of courage, said, "Two things are necessary to succeed in Christian work. You must have a place in your heart for the people you work with—and you must find a place in their hearts."[18] I realize any conversation about racialization in America is bigger than black and white. But, in light of SBC history, each contributor demonstrated that the greatest infraction on the gospel within our denomination has been between blacks and whites. At the convention's birth Southern Baptist leaders distorted Scripture to justify the southern heritage—destruction of black families through chattel slavery. In a nutshell chattel slavery dismantled the black family each time a child was sold away from his or her parents to the highest bidder. Chattel slavery destroyed the idea of black manhood when fathers lacked proprietary rights to their *own* children. Beatings or death resulted when fathers stood against the racialized system to protect their children from legalized kidnapping. In essence some fathers affirmed the principle, "Give me liberty or give me death." And death for many of these fathers was swift when they modeled biblical manhood. Chattel slavery disfigured the identities of black women, making those of a darker hue feel less than beautiful while extolling the worth of lighter-skinned black women against the other. Divide and conquer was the strategic plan. This, beloved, is the American dilemma.[19] We have the legacy of freedom and bondage in the name of God in the American political economy.

In essence, early American civil laws rested on pseudotheological beliefs which sedated consciences against man-stealing during the bullwhip days.[20] I submit a dual premise based on states rights and racial hierarchy. The former

---

[18] William T. Moore, *His Heart Is Black* (Atlanta: Home Mission Board, 1968).

[19] For more information on the logical inconsistency of vying for freedom while venerating slavery, see Gunnar Myrdal, *An American Dilemma: The Negro Problem and Modern Democracy, vol. 1* (New Brunswick: Transaction Publishers, 1995).

[20] In historical studies African diasporic scholars argue for cultural agency when telling the stories of black suffering on American soil. To those who have never heard enslaved Africans narrate their understanding of "inhuman bondage," to borrow from David Brion Davis, I recommend James Mellon, *Bull Whip Days: The Slaves Remember—an Oral History* (New York: Grove Press, reprinted 2002).

refers to the Tenth Amendment which states, "The powers not delegated to the United States by the Constitution, nor prohibited by it to the States, are reserved to the States respectively, or to the people." The latter envisions structural supremacy based on race.

Racial hierarchy explains how racial mythologies became the scaffolding for creating an ethically unbalanced political economy. From an Afro-sensitive vantage point, calls for defense of states' rights meant that dehumanized African peoples living in the southern portion of the United States in early American history maintained their existence as chattel, enhancing the economic viability of many Anglos in the southern economy. Such economic advantages were protected by sanctioned terrorism on black families in slave states. These families were virtually destroyed through centuries of dehumanization—transatlantic slave trade, hereditary slavery, and Jim Crowism.

Frederick Douglass, an early nineteenth-century African-American abolitionist, was correct in saying, "One man's freedom is another man's bondage" since "every man knows that slavery is not right for him."[21] When slavery becomes your lot, the cry for justice is readily heard. Or, put another way, we see injustice through new eyes when our children are kidnapped, beaten, and displaced.

Humans have an innate ability to distort information for personal gain. That is to say, those who define information for the masses are equally endowed with power to determine its allocation. This intellectual power-brokering is properly termed, according to Molefi Asante, "hierarchical discourse." Asante believes every institution, large or small, has gatekeepers in place to protect the interests of the dominant group. Those in power define what is considered credible or reasonable for the masses. Peter Berger calls this institutional privilege a "plausibility structure." If you create the game, you also define the rules. The writers in this volume announce an amendment to the rules.

---

[21] Frederick Douglass, "What to Slave Is the Fourth of July?"

Conclusion

We are living in chaotic times. Such times require significant sacrifices in order to develop students with clear voices that beckon all peoples to submit to the authority of Scripture rather than embrace an ungodly cultural zeitgeist. Obviously, I am not suggesting contemporary America is any worse than early America for marginalized people. If we read American history through a multiethnic lens, for example, we will likely curtail the oft-repeated rhetoric of living in an "age of unprecedented chaos." American history proves terrorism manifested many faces as citizens pursued their goals by any means necessary. Native Americans, African-Americans, and Asian-Americans suffered under the yoke of white supremacy. There is nothing new under the sun.

The heart of the matter is the matter of the heart. Heart work is hard work. When the gospel changes the heart, transformation is evident to all since the renovation of the heart flows from the inside out. So, if erasing the stain of racism in the SBC causes you to ask, "Are we there yet?" as a brother, I will answer with a prayerful, patient, and positive tone: No, we have not arrived. Christ has not set up his kingdom on earth. May Southern Baptists keep walking and working together to remove the stain of racism from the SBC until he comes! Maranatha!

Why the Stain of Racism Remains in the Southern Baptist Convention: An African-American Pastor's Perspective

W. Dwight McKissic Sr.

The election of Pastor Fred Luter as the first African-American president of the Southern Baptist Convention (SBC) in 2012 incarnated and signified a desire that the SBC be more inclusive and empowering of racial minorities in the future than it has been in the past. Although the roots and DNA of the SBC can be traced back to protecting and promulgating the notion of "biblically sanctioned slavery," white supremacy, black economic exploitation, segregation, and slaveholding missionaries, the current SBC no longer represents any of the aforementioned descriptions.

By the late 1950s, the boards of all six Southern Baptist theological seminaries opened the way for the admission of "Negro" students. The resolution of The Southern Baptist Theological Seminary in Louisville, Kentucky, relative to Negro admission reads as follows:

> Since legal barriers have been removed and because of the
> urgent need of adequate seminary training in the south for

Negro Baptist students who are at present deprived of proper
theological education, that beginning with the session 1951–52
carefully selected Negroes be admitted [as] candidates for the B.D.,
Th.M. or Th.D. [and] to classes, library, and all academic rights
and privileges.[1]

Considering the blatant racist roots of the SBC, this resolution represents
serious and substantial progress. However, the phrase "carefully selected
Negroes" reeks with racism and was indicative of the prevalent SBC mind-set
of that era, which generally regarded persons of African descent as inferior.
Consequently, only "carefully selected Negroes" would be admitted to SBC
seminaries.

Standing in the room with more than 7,000 people when Luter was
elected, one could feel the intensity, authenticity, and repentance (heart
change) concerning race on the part of most SBC messengers present. This is
no longer the SBC of the white supremacist grandfather or of Bull Connor.

However, currently, the stain and residue of racism remains in the SBC.
In the past twenty years we have seen white Southern Baptist churches deny
baptismal rites and marriage rites to black congregants. We have seen a
deceased biracial child denied burial rites at a white Southern Baptist church
cemetery. We have seen an SBC missionary couple denied a speaking opportunity at a white Southern Baptist church in Louisiana when it was discovered that their family had adopted a black child. I sat on a missions funding
committee for the Baptist General Convention of Texas in the mid-90s when
it was discovered that all black-affiliated Texas Baptist churches were categorically paying 6 percent interest on loans granted by the committee while
white and Hispanic churches were paying 0 percent interest loans.

Noticeably absent initially was an African-American from the mega-
important Great Commission Task Force of the SBC appointed in 2009.

---

[1] *The Christian Century*, April 11, 1951.

Noticeably absent from a 2015 Midwestern Seminary symposium on "The SBC & the 21st Century" was an African-American presenter. All SBC entity heads remain white currently. We have come a long way, but we still have a long way to go.

Succinctly as possible, I want to list five reasons the stain of racism remains in the SBC.

1. Racism in the larger society influences systems and individuals in SBC life.

2. The belief held by many in the SBC that racism in today's world is a myth actually perpetuates racism. If one believes racism is a myth, that person has to dismiss, deny, downgrade, diffuse, or redirect even obvious acts of racism. The fact that the editors and publisher of this book are willing to acknowledge racism in the SBC is a significant step forward in improving race relations in the SBC.

3. Unrepentant teaching regarding the curse of Ham theory, though relatively uncommon today, nonetheless persists and contributes to the stain of racism in the SBC.

The 1995 SBC resolution on racial reconciliation certainly was the right and needed response to the convention's racist past. Yet the curse of Ham theory that provided theological license to Southern Baptists and society at large to practice slavery and segregation was not acknowledged or repented of in the '95 document. False teaching on the curse of Ham was the root of the racist tree in SBC life. We must lay the axe at the root of the tree if we want to eradicate racism completely in the SBC.

4. The implication that all persons in the Bible were white continues to promote racism in the SBC, even when that implication is unintentional. Because the SBC has historically neglected and still neglects to teach about people of color—including Africans/blacks—who played significant roles in the Old and New Testaments, many Southern Baptists view biblical characters as being white, including Jesus. The belief that all biblical characters

are white can lead to a conscious or subconscious conclusion that whites are superior to people of color. That mind-set can work its way into management decisions in the SBC.

Because SBC seminaries have not traditionally trained seminarians concerning the prominence of people of color—including Africans/blacks—in the Bible, Southern Baptists in the pew are also largely unaware. This ignorance is perpetuated by the fact that our SBC seminaries have few black or brown faculty members and by the additional facts that most SBC seminaries either only or mainly require books written by white men, primarily feature white guest preachers, and primarily feature white lecturers for special conferences.

In a February 2015 chapel message at The Southern Baptist Theological Seminary addressing "The Table of the Nations, the Tower of Babel, and the Marriage Supper of the Lamb: Ethnic Diversity and the Radical Vision of the Gospel of Jesus Christ," R. Albert Mohler Jr. stated, "African and Asiatic people may well be rooted in the sons of Ham." It is rare that a white Southern Baptist—particularly with academic pedigree—would affirm an African/black presence in Scripture to that magnitude. The implications of his statement are staggering. It places Hamitic peoples/Africans in the bloodline of Jesus and underscores their prominence in the Old Testament. SBC seminary students need to hear more of this perspective and read more books written by black, brown, and white authors with this perspective. It would do wonders for race relations.

Fifth, the false belief of many blacks that black people cannot be racist because we are supposedly powerless to practice racism is a reason the stain of racism remains in the SBC. Racism is a sin. And there is no sin black people are incapable of committing, including racism. No one race has a monopoly on racism. To the extent that blacks can practice racism toward others and display racist attitudes, we too have been, and sometimes are, guilty. The distrust, bitterness, lack of forgiveness, and offensive/racist language directed by blacks toward whites are sometimes rooted in an unrepentant attitude toward our own racism. We cannot expect race relations in the SBC to improve until we, as a race, are willing to repent of our own racial prejudice. All ethnic groups must take responsibility to improve race relations in the SBC and to remove the stain of racism from all aspects of SBC life.

Why the Stain of Racism Remains in the Southern Baptist Convention: An Anglo Seminary President's Perspective

DANIEL L. AKIN

As I sit down to write this epilogue and reflect on my assignment, I cannot do so without mixed emotions. On the one hand, I am more hopeful and optimistic than I have ever been in my lifetime when it comes to racial progress and reconciliation in the Southern Baptist Convention (SBC). By God's grace and work in our midst, we are not where we were in 1845, 1925, 1960, or even 2000. In my lifetime (I was born in 1957) I have seen significant change and advance in the SBC. Today our churches look a whole lot more like the church in heaven than they have at any time in our history. In this we can rejoice.

However, a dark cloud hovers over our nation and also over our convention of churches. Do the names Trevon Martin, Michael Brown, Eric Garner, Walter Scott, Samuel De Bose, and Sandra Bland sound familiar? They should. Who among us will ever forget the Emanuel African Methodist Episcopal Church massacre of June 17, 2015, when nine brothers and sisters were gunned down simply because they were black? Follow that up with the Confederate flag controversy, with many white Southern Baptists coming out in its defense publicly and privately, and the undeniable fact that most of our churches remain decidedly segregated and predominately white. The sin of racism remains in the SBC, and we are still a long way away from what God redeemed his church to be. So this question must be asked: why does the stain of racism remain in the SBC?

Why the Stain Remains

The simplest and most basic answer is our depravity and sin. Even though those of us who have been redeemed by the blood of Christ are new creations in him (2 Cor 5:17), our journey of sanctification is a long and difficult one. Vestiges of our fallen nature remain, and we are in desperate need of the Spirit and Word to work out sanctification in our lives. Some redeemed Southern Baptists have deep roots in racism, segregation, bigotry, and prejudice. These roots are not easily pulled, and until they are, their ugly fruit will remain. The taint of our depravity continues to soil our convention.

A second reason the stain remains is unregenerate church membership. This is a sad but undeniable fact. Too many people who have their names on church rolls have never been truly converted. They have never been born again (John 3). That they would continue to think and act like unbelievers should not surprise us. It is inevitable and natural. Unbelievers will always act like unbelievers.

Third, too many Southern Baptist churches have been seduced by their cultural context, especially in the Deep South. In a spirit of full disclosure, I grew up in Georgia and now reside in North Carolina. I have experiential knowledge of what I am saying. What you often find is not an active and aggressive racism so much as a passive and indifferent racism. I gather with my tribe and, of course, my tribe tends to look a whole lot like me. People of different ethnicities are certainly welcome to join us on our terms, adapting to our context and way of doing things. However, don't expect us to change. Change is the responsibility of the others.

Fourth, overcoming racism requires humility and sacrifice of the majority race, virtues that do not come easily. You see, welcoming you into my community on my terms is one thing. But to surrender my preferences so that you feel at home in what is now our community is something more. But let me go further. Even more humility and sacrifice are needed for me to invite you to the table of leadership and to welcome you to sit at the head of the table. Until we can arrive at this God-ordained destination, our convention of churches will struggle to receive the full blessing of God and attain credibility with a cynical and skeptical culture that already questions the authenticity of our faith. Racism and bigotry make us easy targets for hostile arrows.

A Personal Word from My Heart

As I noted earlier, I am a son of the South, having been born and raised in Atlanta, Georgia. I love and appreciate many aspects of that culture. However, other characteristics of Southern heritage cause me sorrow and grief.

I remember when schools were integrated. I was in the fifth grade. "Now," some (too many) said, "my children are going to be forced to go to school with 'n—s.'" I remember when Martin Luther King Jr. was murdered, and people said, "I'm glad that 'n—r' is dead." I remember when a black man visited our all-white church and, even as a boy, I could tell he was not welcome and that people hoped he would not return. Interracial dating was not even on the radar screen. Adopting children not of your ethnicity was not even a consideration. And later, when I served as dean of students at Southeastern Baptist Theological Seminary (1992–1996), a school that is making significant progress in welcoming and increasing its ethnic population among students and staff, I remember a student pastor being fired for leading black children to Christ and inviting them to join the church. I remember. . . .

But I also have other memories. I remember the black family whose farm was next door to my grandparents' farm. I remember going over and playing with the children who lived there just as I played with my white neighbors. Neither I nor my parents or grandparents gave it a second thought. I remember the black mother on that farm, a lady I called "Aunt Loraine," who hugged me and loved on me and fed me like I was one of her own. I remember my mom picking up a big, black, teenage football player friend of mine named Danny Pounds and giving him a ride to a game because he was in a walking cast following knee surgery. When she was asked why she did such a thing, she simply said, "He is my son's friend and he needed a ride." I remember fondly my athletic teammates like Andre Greer, Derrick Stokes, Willie Ellis, William Smith, Jack Bodie, Willie Nunley, and Joe Malone, all of whom were black and all of whom I gladly called my friends. They were genuine friends who just happened to be black.

I remember even as a boy that though I was proud to be from the South, played football in "Tara" stadium (a reference to *Gone with the Wind*), and marveled at the granite portraits of Robert E. Lee, Stonewall Jackson, and Jefferson Davis on the side of Stone Mountain, I was never comfortable with the Confederate flag—never! Oh, I could understand how it recalled the bravery and courage of soldiers from the South during the Civil War. However, I could never escape the reality that for many others it conjured up memoires and nightmares of slavery, oppression, murder, lynchings, rape, broken families, and tortured lives. It seems no small sacrifice to place such an item inside a museum rather than on a flagpole. The shame and pain it causes for too many people far outweighs its reference to bravery and courage. That this was even a point of debate or question for followers of Jesus within the SBC is evidence of our sinfulness and the occasion of our shame. To set aside such a small thing—and it is a small thing—for love of my black brothers and sisters and the cause of the gospel seems like a no-brainer to me. In saying this, I make no claim to moral or spiritual superiority in my thoughts on these matters. I know better than anyone the depths of my depravity, the bigotries of my heart, and my moment-by-moment need of God's grace, wisdom, and transforming power. Paul's category "chief of sinners" is one I am familiar with on a personal level. But I know that a stain of racism remains in the SBC, and I want to continue to do my part as a leader within the SBC to erase that stain.

Conclusion

In sum, racism is not a surface issue in the SBC, though it often manifests itself in surface and public ways. No, it is an issue of the soul. Its root and source is the sinful, evil, and wicked human heart that fails to recognize we are all created in the image of God and that beneath the surface, deep down where it really counts, we are all the same. Ideologies of hate are more than skin deep. They drill down to the depths of our being. Let Jesus change our hearts, and he will change our lives. Let Jesus change our lives, and he will change our churches. Let Jesus change our churches, and he will change our witness. When people see how we love one another without discrimination or distinction, then they will know we belong to him. After all, because of a bloody cross and an empty tomb, we all have the same "Daddy," we confess the same Savior, and we are indwelt by the same Spirit. We are family. By God's grace, for his glory, and for our good, let's live like it in the SBC!

Southern Baptists Can Remove the Stain of Racism from the Southern Baptist Convention

T. Vaughn Walker

The recognition that every individual addresses the complex issues of life from his or her own particular perspective and context is critical in consideration of a topic such as racism. Racial privilege, racism (overt and covert), sexism, and classism have impacted and to differing degrees still impact the lives of the people groups that comprise the largest and "most diverse" Protestant Christian denomination on earth—the Southern Baptist Convention (SBC).

I come from the perspective of one who has been officially connected to the SBC since the mid-1970s and was the first African-American to be appointed to the faculty at any SBC seminary. I grew up in a rural, almost totally segregated Virginia community, graduated from high school in that same community as one of only two African-Americans in my senior class, later united with a local Southern Baptist congregation in Oregon, along with my wife, as their first African-American members, and ultimately served as a Sunday school teacher and deacon in that congregation. These experiences provide further context for my perspective as an African-American pastor and professor in the SBC. As one of four African-American professors at Southern Seminary, I have had the grand privilege for nearly thirty years of teaching and supervising men and women of many races, nationalities, and cultural backgrounds as they prepare to serve Christ. At the same time I have served as senior pastor of the same local congregation for more than three decades, a congregation which today is more racially and culturally diverse than at any time in its 105-year history.

I grew up in a church that was 100 percent African-American and cooperated with both the Lott Carey Baptist Convention and the National Baptist Convention, USA, Inc. Our church had no persons of other races. Marriage between black and white individuals was illegal in Virginia during my childhood years. Occasionally white people would visit our small church, especially if they were guests from out of town. Whites who visited were always warmly greeted by all in the congregation. More frequently, white individuals would attend the funerals, and I assume some of the weddings, of African-Americans who worked with or for them. Almost all funerals and a vast majority of the African-American community's weddings were held in church facilities, even when the individuals involved were not officially members of the congregation.

As I recall, the vast majority of white Baptist congregations in our community were Southern Baptist. One white Baptist church cooperated with both the SBC and the American Baptist Convention (ABC). I believe at least one congregation cooperated only with the ABC, and a small representation of Baptists were identified as Independent Baptist, Free Will Baptist, and Primitive Baptist. During those times I do not recall any black Baptist congregations cooperating with the SBC, though historians say some did just that beginning in 1951, and more followed suit beginning in the 1960s.[1] Most black Baptists were Lott Carey affiliated as well as aligned with one of three National Baptist Convention bodies, namely the National Baptist Convention, USA, Inc., the National Baptist Convention of America, and the Progressive National Baptist Convention. A couple of African-American Baptist churches cooperated with the ABC for the benefit packages available to clergy not available in the National Baptist bodies. In the years following my childhood, some historic African-American congregations cooperated with the SBC, and presently some church plants are only SBC connected. Mark Croston, then senior pastor of the East End Baptist Church of Suffolk, Virginia, in recent years held the distinction of serving simultaneously as state convention president of a convention in cooperation with the SBC and also as state president of one of the National Baptist-affiliated state bodies.

In my adult years in Missouri and Kentucky, the preferred approach for addressing racial reconciliation among white and black Baptists was through programs designated as "cooperative ministries." National and state Baptist leaders as well as local churches and district associations attempted to strengthen the Baptist witness as well as enhance racial reconciliation by calling for acts of cooperation across all levels of Baptist life. Local churches (black and white) held pulpit-exchange services, often during Black History Month. Missions outreach efforts such as the Baptist Fellowship Center (BFC) in Louisville, Kentucky, were models for the nation. The BFC was jointly sponsored by the then Home Mission Board of the SBC (now the North American Mission Board), the Kentucky Baptist Convention, the Long Run Baptist Association, and the General Association of Kentucky

---

[1] Sid Smith, "Black Church Growth as Denominational Alignment," *Ethnicity*, January/February 1985, 1. Everett Hullum, "On a Path Toward Reconciliation: National and Southern Baptists Begin Moves to Increase Cooperative Endeavors," *Ethnicity*, Spring 1984, 2. Emmanuel McCall, "From 1350 Spring St.," *Ethnicity*, March/April 1985, 2.

Baptists (including the Central District Baptist Association). Black and white Baptists worked side by side in ministry opportunities focused primarily on the disadvantaged within all races. Summer missionaries and church mission teams frequented the center, which offered hands-on mission experiences primarily to high school and college students across racial lines.

The SBC supplied funding to the American Baptist College in Nashville, Tennessee (NBC, USA, Inc., affiliated), well into the 1980s. American Baptist College, Simmons Bible College (now Simmons College of Kentucky), and Bishop College in Texas were historically African-American institutions that supplied significant numbers of African-American, African, and Caribbean students to SBC seminaries. Some people referred to Southern Seminary unofficially as the largest black seminary in the nation because of its large enrollment of African-Americans in the 1970s through 1990s.[2] Many of today's most successful African-American leaders in the local church, SBC denominational staffs, and missions organizations owe at least part of their preparation to SBC seminaries. Many of these individuals have become important leaders for racial and ethnic reconciliation in communities where they now serve as well as nationally and internationally.

We must resist the temptation to deny, ignore, or even minimize the reality that a stain of racism still permeates our culture and our Christian landscape. But to argue that there has been little or no improvement or advancement in genuine reconciliation is to fail to appreciate the transforming power of the

---

[2] The designation was not technically correct. For instance, during the 1980–1981 academic year, Southern did have more than fifty black students enrolled (*Thirtieth Annual Report to the Board of Trustees of the Southern Baptist Theological Seminary*, Student Statistical Report Fall 1971–Spring 1981, C-50, Archives, The Southern Baptist Theological Seminary, Louisville, Kentucky). However, two of the largest historically black seminaries in America, Virginia Union University Divinity School and Howard University Divinity School both had more total students in 1980–1981 than Southern Seminary had black students (Association of Theological Schools in the United States and Canada, *Fact Book on Theological Education 1980–1981*, ed. Marvin J. Taylor [Vandalia, OH: Association of Theological Schools, 1981], 53, 56).

Holy Spirit in the lives and hearts of men and women of faith. When one removes the sociopolitical chatter and begins to focus on a clear biblical and theological framework, genuine Christians—black and white, the SBC and NBC, as well as others—are uniting around the call of Christ for reconciliation to him and among one another as never before in our history. First John 4:7–11 offers compelling words to all believers in Christ:

> Dear friends, let us love one another, because love is from God, and everyone who loves has been born of God and knows God. The one who does not love does not know God, because God is love. God's love was revealed among us in this way: God sent His One and Only Son into the world so that we might live through Him. Love consists in this: not that we loved God, but that He loved us and sent His Son to be the propitiation for our sins. Dear friends, if God loved us in this way, we also must love one another.

He who does not love does not know God! May Southern Baptists, and all Christians throughout the world, continue to work together to remove the dark stain of racism from the SBC.

Appendix 1

Suggested Reading List on Race and Race Relations

Abdul-Jabbar, Kareem, and Alan Steinberg. *Black Profiles in Courage: A Legacy of African American Achievement*. New York: William Morrow, 1996.

Alcántara, Jared E. *Crossover Preaching: Intercultural-Improvisational Homiletics in Conversation with Gardner C. Taylor*. Downers Grove: InterVarsity, 2015.

Alexander, Michelle. *The New Jim Crow: Mass Incarceration in the Age of Colorblindness*. New York: Perseus Distribution, 2010.

Anyabwile, Thabiti. *Reviving the Black Church*. Nashville: B&H, 2015.

———. *Decline of African-American Theology: From Biblical Faith to Cultural Captivity*. Downers Grove: InterVarsity, 2007.

Ammi, Ben. *God, the Black Man and Truth*. Washington, DC: Commnication Press, 1990.

Anderson, Wayne. *Plessy v. Ferguson: Legalizing Segregation*. New York: Rosen Publishing, 2004.

Angelou, Maya. *I Know Why the Caged Bird Sings*. New York: Random House, 1969.

Ani, Marimba. *Yurugu: An African-Centered Critique of European Cultural Thought and Behavior*. Trenton: Africasn World Press, 1994.

Bell, Janet Cheatham. *Till Victory Is Won: Famous Black Quotations from the NAAC*. New York: Pocket Books, 2002.

Boyle, Kevin. *Arc of Justice: A Saga of Race, Civil Rights, and Murder in the Jazz Age*. New York: Henry Holt, 2004.

Bradley, Anthony J. *Aliens in the Promised Land: Why Minority Leadership Is Overlooked in White Christian Churches and Institutions.* Phillipsburg: P&R, 2013.

————. *Black Scholars in White Space: New Vistas in African-American Studies from the Christian Academy.* Eugene: Pickwick, 2015.

————. *Keep Your Head Up: America's New Black Christian Leaders, Social Consciousness, and the Cosby Conversation.* Wheaton: Crossway, 2012.

Brown, Tony. *What Mama Taught Me.* New York: William Morrow, 2003.

Carter, Anthony J. *On Being Black and Reformed: A New Perspective on the African-American Christian Experience.* Phillipsburg: P&R Publishing, 2003.

Carter, Anthony J, and Ken Jones. *Glory Road: the Journeys of 10 African-Americans into Reformed Christianity.* Wheaton: Crossway Books, 2009.

Cleveland, Christena. *Disunity in Christ: Uncovering the Hidden Forces that Keep Us Apart.* Downers Grove: InterVarsity Press, 2013.

Cose, Ellis. *The Envy of the World: on Being a Black Man in America.* New York: Washington Square Press, 2002.

Cross, Haman, Donna E. Scott, and Eugene Seals. *What's Up with Malcolm?: the Real Failure of Islam.* Chicago: Moody Press, 1993.

Douglass, Frederick. *The Most Complete Collection of His Written Works and Speeches.* New York: Northpointe Classics, 2011.

Du Bois, W. E. B. *The Souls of Black Folk: Essays and Sketches.* Charlottesville: University of Virginia Library, 1996.

————. *The Talented Tenth.* New York: James Pott and Co., 1903.

Dunbar, Paul Lawrence, and William Dean Howells. *The Complete Poems of Paul Lawrence Dunbar.* Dodd, Mead, 1896.

Dungy, Tony, and Nathan Whitacker. *The Mentor Leader.* Carol Stream: Tyndale House, 2010.

Edwards, Korie L. *The Elusive Dream: The Power of Race in Interracial Churches.* New York: Oxford University Press, 2008.

Ellis, Carl F. *Free at Last? The Gospel and the African-American Experience.* Downers Grove: InterVarsity Press, 1986.

Ellis, Carl F, Don Davis, and R. C. Smith. *S.O.S., Saving Our Sons: Confronting the Lure of Islam with Truth, Faith & Courage.* New York: Imani Books, 2007.

Ellison, Ralph, and John F Callahan. *Juneteenth: a Novel.* New York: Random House, 1999.

Fergus, Edward, Pedro Noguera, and Margary Martin. *Schooling for Resilience: Improving the Life Trajectory of Black and Latino Boys.* Cambridge: Harvard Education Press, 2014.

Gilbert, Olive, and Sojourner Truth. *Narrative of Sojourner Truth.* Champaigne: Project Gutenberg, 2000.

Glymph, Thavolia. *Out of the House of Bondage: The Transformation of the Plantation Household.* Cambridge: Cambridge University Press, 2008.

Gomez, Michael Angelo. *Exchanging Our Country Marks: The Transformation of African Identities in the Colonial and Antebellum South.* Chapel Hill: University of North Carolina Press, 1998.

Hardin, John A. *Fifty Years of Segregation: Black Higher Education in Kentucky, 1904–1954.* Lexington: University of Kentucky Press, 1997.

Harris, Leslie M. *In the Shadow of Slavery: African Americans in New York City, 1626–1863.* Chicago: University of Chicago Press, 2003.

Harris, Michael D. *Colored Picture.* Chapel Hill: University of North Carolina Press, 2003.

Haynes, Lemuel, and Richard Newman. *Black Preacher to White America: The Collected Writings of Lemuel Haynes, 1774–1833.* Brooklyn: Carlson Publishing, 1990.

Haynes, Stephen R. *The Last Segregated Hour: The Memphis Kneel-ins and the Campaign for Southern Church Desegregation.* New York: Oxford University Press, 2012.

Holloway, Jonathan Scott. *Confronting the Veil: Abram Harris, Jr., E. Franklin Frazier, and Ralph Bunche, 1919–1941*. Chapel Hill: University of North Carolina Press, 2002.

Holt, Thomas C. *Children of Fire: A History of African Americans*. New York: Hill and Wang, 2010.

Hurston, Zora Neale. *Their Eyes Were Watching God: A Novel*. New York: Perennial Library, 1990.

Johnson, Walter. *Soul by Soul: Life Inside the Antebellum Slave Market*. Cambridge: Harvard University Press, 1999.

Jordan, Winthrop D. *The White Man's Burden: Historical Origins of Racism in the United States*. New York: Oxford University Press, 1974.

King, C Richard, and Charles Fruehling Springwood. *Beyond the Cheers: Race as a Spectacle in College Sports*. Albany: State University of New York Press, 2001.

King, Martin Luther, Jr., Clayborne Carson, and Peter Holloran. *A Knock at Midnight: Inspiration from the Great Sermons of Reverend Martin Luther King, Jr.* New York: Intellectual Properties Management in association with Warner Books, 1998.

Kunjufu, Juwanza. *Countering the Conspiracy to Destroy Black Boys*. Chicago: Afro-Am Publishing, 1983–1995.

———. *Motivating and Preparing Black Youth for Success*. Chicago: African American Images, 1986.

———. *A Talk with Jawanza: Critical Issues in Educating African American Youth*. Chicago: African American Images, 1989.

Kuykendall, Crystal. *From Rage to Hoper: Strategies for Reclaiming Black & Hispanic Students*. Bloomington: National Educational Service, 1992.

Lewis, David L. *W. E. B. Du Bois*. New York: Henry Holt, 1993–2000.

Madhubuti, Haki R. *Tough Notes: A Healing Call for Creating Exceptional Black Men: Affirmations, Meditations, Readings, and Strategies*. Chicago: Third World Press, 2002.

Majors, Richard, and Janet Mancini Billson. *Cool Pose: The Dilemmas of Black Manhood in America.* New York: Macmillan, 1992.

Medina, Tony. *No Noose Is Good Noose.* New York: Writers and Readers Publishing, 1996.

Mitchell, Michele. *Righteous Propagation: African Americans and the Politics of Racial Destiny After Reconstruction.* Chapel Hill: University of North Carolina Press, 2004.

Model, Suzanne. *West Indian Immigrants: A Black Success Story?* New York: Russell Sage Foundation, 2008.

Ogbar, Jeffrey Ogbonna Green. *Black Power: Radical Politics and African American Identity.* Baltimore: Johns Hopkins University Press, 2004.

Payne, Charles. *I've Got the Light of Freedom: The Organizing Tradition and the Mississippi Freedom Struggle.* Berkeley: University of Californina Press, 1995.

Perry, Theresa, Claude Steele, and Asa G Hilliard. *Young Gifted and Black: Promoting High Achievement Among African-American Students.* Boston: Beacon, 2003.

Reder, Diane Proctor. *Elijah's Mantle: Empowering the Next Generation of African American Christian Leaders.* Grand Rapids: Kregal, 2013.

Redmond, Eric C. *Where Are All the Brothers? Straight Answers to Men's Questions About the Church.* Wheaton: Crossway Books, 2008.

Sammons, Jeffrey T, and John Howard Morrow. *Harlem's Rattlers and the Great War: The Undaunted 369th Regiment & the African American Quest for Equality.* Lawrence: University Press of Kansas, 2014.

Scott, Rebecca J. *Degrees of Freedom: Louisiana and Cuba After Slavery.* Cambridge: Belknap Press of Harvard University Press, 2005.

Shabazz, Ilyasah, and Kim McLarin. *Growing Up X.* New York: One World/ Ballantine, 2002.

Skinner, Tom. *Black and Free.* Grand Rapids: Zondervan, 1968.

Smith, Gerald L. *A Black Educator in the Segregated South: Kentucky's Rufus B. Atwood*. Lexington: University of Kentucky Press, 1994.

Stevenson, Bryan. *Just Mercy: A Story of Justice and Redemption*. New York: Spiegel & Grau, 2014.

Tatum, Alfred. *Teaching Reading to Black Adolescent Males: Closing the Achievement Gap*. Portland: Stenhouse Publishers, 2005.

Tatum, Beverly Daniel. *Why Are All the Black Kids Sitting Together in the Cafeteria? Conversations About Race*. New York: BasicBooks, 1997.

Thompson-Miller, Ruth, Joe R. Feagin, and Leslie Houts Picca. *Jim Crow's Legacy: The Lasting Impact of Segregation*. New York: Rowman & Littlefield, 2015.

Walker, Alice. *The Color Purple: A Novel*. New York: Harcourt Brace Jovanovich, 1982.

Wells, H. G. *The Invisible Man*. Charlottesville: University of Virginia Library, 1995.

West, Cornell. *Race Matters*. Boton: Beacon Press, 1993.

Williams, Jarvis J. *Christ Died for Our Sins: Representation and Substitution in Romans and Their Jewish Martyrological Background*. Eugene: Pickwick, 2015.

———. *For Whom Did Christ Die? The Extent of the Atonement in Paul*. Paternoster Biblical Monographs Series. Milton Keynes: Paternoster, 2012.

———. *One New Man: The Cross and Racial Reconciliation in Pauline Theology*. Nashville: B&H, 2010.

Woodson, Carter G. *The Mis-education of the Negro*. Trenten: Africa World Press, 1990.

Wright, Richard. *Native Son*. New York: Harper, 1940.

X, Malcolm, and Alex Haley. *The Autobiography of Malcolm X*. New York: Grove Press, 1965.

Books for Children and Youth

Adoff, Arnold, and Benny Andrews. *I Am the Darker Brother: An Anthology of Modern Poems by African Americans*. New York: Aladdin Paperbacks, 1997.

Allen, Debbie, and Kadir Nelson. *Dancing in the Wing*. New York: Dial Books for Young Readers, 2000.

Asim, Jabari. *The Road to Freedom: A Story of the Reconstruction*. Columbus: Waterbird Books, 2004.

Asim, Jabari, and LeUyen Pham. *Whose Toes Are Those?* New York: Little, Brown, 2006.

Barber, Tiki, Ronde Barber, Robert Burleigh, and Barry Root. *By My Brother's Side*. New York: Simon & Schuster Books for Young Readers, 2004.

Barton, Chris, and Don Tate. *The Amazing Age of John Roy Lynch*. Grand Rapids: Eerdmans Books for Young Readers, 2015.

Bolden, Tonya. *Cause: Reconstruction America, 1863–1877*. New York: Knopf, 2005.

Bolden, Tonya, and R. Gregory Christie. *The Champ: The Story of Muhammad Ali*. New York: Dragonfly Books, 2007.

Bridges, Ruby. *Ruby Bridges Goes to School: My True Story*. New York: Scholastic, 2009.

Cameron, Ann, and Diane Worfolk Allison. *Julian, Secret Agent*. New York: Random House, 1988.

Chambers, Veronica, and Paul Lee. *Amistad Rising: A Story of Freedom*. San Diego: Harcourt Brace, 1998.

Cline-Ransome, Lesa. *Satchel Paige*. New York: Simon & Schuster Books for Young Readers, 2000.

Cooke, Trish, and Paul Howard. *Full, Full, Full of Love*. Cambridge: Candlewick Press, 2003.

Cooke, Trish, and Helen Oxenbury. *So Much*. Cambridge: Candlewick Press, 1994.

Curtis, Christopher Paul. *Bud, Not Buddy*. New York: Delacorte Press, 1999.

Dungy, Tony, and Amy June Bates. *You Can Do It!* New York: Simon & Schuster; London: Turnaround, 2008.

Greene, Meg. *Into the Land of Freedom: African Americans in Reconstruction*. Minneapolis: Lerner Publications, 2004.

Greenfield, Eloise, and Floyd Cooper. *Grandpa's Face*. New York: Philomel Books, 1998.

Hakim, Joy. *Reconstruction and Reform*. New York: Oxford University Press, 1994.

Hansen, Joyce. *Bury Me Not in a Land of Slaves: African-Americans in the Time of Reconstruction*. Danbury: F. Watts, 2000.

Hoffman, Mary, and Caroline Binch. *Amazing Grace*. New York: Dial Books for Young Readers, 1991.

Hopkinson, Deborah. *Sweet Clara and the Freedo Quilt*. New York: Knopf, 1993.

Hudson, Wade, and Valerie Wilson Wesley. *Afro Bets Book of Black Heroes*. City of Orange: Just Us Books, 2013.

Johnson, Angela, and Rhonda Mitchell. *Daddy Calls Me Man*. New York: Orchard Books, 1997.

Jordan, Roslyn, Deloris Jordan, and Kadir Nelson. *Salt in His Shoes: Michael Jordan in Pursuit of a Dream*. New York: Simon & Schuster Books for Young Readers, 2000.

Kamerman, Sylvia E. *Plays of Black Americans: Episodes from the Black Experience in America, Dramatized for Young People*. Boston: Plays, 1987.

Katz, Karen. *The Color of Us*. New York: Henry Holt, 1999.

Keats, Ezra Jack. *The Snowy Day*. New York: Viking Press, 1962.

Krull, Kathleen, and David Diaz. *Wilma Unlimited: How Wilma Rudolph Became the World's Fastest Woman*. San Diego: Harcourt Brace, 1996.

Lee, Spike, Tonya Lewis Lee, and Kadir Nelson. *Please, Puppy, Please*. New York: Simon & Schuster Books for Young Readers, 2005.

Levine, Ellen, and Kadir Nelson. *Henry's Freedom Box*. New York: Scholastic Press, 2007.

Lorbiecki, Marybeth, and K. Wendy Popp. *Sister Anne's Hands*. New York: Dial Books for Young Readers, 1998.

Marzollo, Jean, and Ken Wilson-Max. *The Little Plant Doctor: A Story About George Washington Carver*. New York: Holiday House, 2011.

McAdam, Doug. *Freedom Summer*. New York: Oxford University Press, 1988.

McKissack, Pat, and Jerry Pinkney. *Goin' Someplace Special*. New York: Atheneum Books for Young Readers, 2001.

McKissack, Pat, Rachel Isadora, and Fred Weinberg. *Flossie and the Fox*. New York: Weston Woods Studios: Scholastic, 2002.

McPherson, James M. *Into the West: From Reconstruction to the Final Days of the American Frontier*. New York: Atheneum Books for Young Readers, 2006.

Meltzer, Brad, and Chris Eliopoulos. *I Am Jackie Robinson*. New York: Dial Books for Young Readers, an imprint of Penguin Group, 2015.

Mettger, Zak. *Reconstruction: America After the Civil War*. New York: Lodestar Books, 1994.

Moore, Eva. *The Story of George Washington Carver*. New York: Scholastic, 1971.

Myers, Walter Dean, and Christopher Myers. *Monster*. New York: HarperCollins, 1999.

Nelson, Kadir. *He's Got the Whole World in His Hands*. New York: Dial Books for Young Readers, 2005.

———. *We Are the Ship: The Story of Negro League Baseball*. New York: Jump at the Sun/Hyperion Books for Children, 2008.

Osborne, Linda Barrett. *Traveling the Freedom Road: From Slavery and the Civil War Through Reconstruction*. New York: Abrams Books for Young Readers, 2009.

Perritano, John. *Free at Last!* St. Catharines, Ontario: Crabtree, 2009.

Ringgold, Faith. *Aunt Harriet's Underground Railroad in the Sky*. New York: Crown Publishers, 1992.

———. *Tar Beach*. New York: Crown Publishers, 1991.

Ruggiero, Adriane. *Reconstruction*. New York: Marshall Cavendish Benchmark, 2007.

Ryan, Pam Munoz, and Brian Selznick. *When Marian Sang: The True Recital of Marian Anderson*. New York: Scholastic Press, 2002.

Smalls, Irene, and Michael Hays. *Kevin and His Dad*. Boston: Little, Brown, 1999.

Steptoe, John, and John Stevens. *Mufaro's Beautiful Daughters: An African Tale*. New York: Lothrop, Lee & Shepard Books, 1987.

Stout, Glenn. *Jackie Robinson*. New York: Little, Brown, 2006.

Swain-Bates, Crystal, and Megan Bair. *Big Hair, Don't Care*. Walnut: Goldest Karat Publishing, 2013.

Tarpley, Natasha, and Earl B Lewis. *I Love My Hair!* Boston: Little, Brown, 1998.

Taylor, Mildred D, and Michael Hays. *The Gold Cadillac*. New York: Dial Books for Young Readers, 1987.

Tyler, Michael, and David Lee Csicsko. *The Skin You Live In*. Chicago: Chicago Children's Museum, 2005.

Weatherford, Carole Boston, and Jerome Lagarrigue. *Freedom on the Menu: The Greensboro Sit-ins*. New York: Dial Books for Young Readers, 2005.

Weatherford, Carole Boston, and Kadir Nelson. *Moses: When Harriet Tubman Led Her People to Freedom*. New York: Hyperion Books for Children, 2006.

Wiles, Deborah. *Revolution*. New York: Scholastic, 2014.

Winston, Sherri. *President of the Whole Sixth Grade*. Boston: Little, Brown Books for Young Readers, 2015.

Yarbrough, Camille, and Carole M Byard. *Cornrows*. New York: Coward, McCann & Geoghegan, 1979.

Sample Syllabus for Introduction to African-American History

Title:	Introduction to African-American History
Semester:	Spring XXXX
Instructor:	Instructor's Name Office: XXXXXXXX
E-mail: XXXXXXX	Office Hours: Days and Times
Tel: XXX-XXX-XXXX	T.A.: Assistant's Name

Purpose

The purpose of this course is to introduce participants to the history of African-Americans broadly. The course will introduce material and provide foundational support to individuals with limited proficiency in African-American history. Many of the required works in the course are classics. The objective of the course is to help one understand history broadly and ask questions that will enhance further study of this subject. Throughout the course we will discuss the readings. All participants are expected to read and contribute to classroom discussions.

Upon successful completion of the requirements of this course, students will:

1. Be exposed to a broad range of reading material and discussions on race.

2. Cultivate spiritual and moral well-being on race relations through exposure to the literature.

3. Develop a teaching from a selected book.

4. Articulate a historical understanding of the African-American experience.

5. Be able to articulate how the course readings and lectures fit together.

6. Be able to articulate how once overlooked, neglected, and absent voices fit into their previous knowledge.

Course Requirements

Four Critical Essays

The purpose of each essay is to assess the writer's ability to present a rational and accurate historical argument. Each paper will be five to six pages in length and will be graded based on the following criteria.

1. A summary of the work

2. Argument to include the strengths and weaknesses of the works

3. Comparison of two works

4. How the book challenged or supported one's previous understanding of the African-American experience

5. How to use the material in a practical sense in the future

Presentation of Research

Students will present one of the above-mentioned research papers to the class. A development of the course schedule for presentation will take place during the second week of class. Students will develop discussion questions. These questions will guide classmates in discussion following each paper's presentation.

Participation in Discussion

Each student must contribute constructive feedback to each presenter. These comments must include, but are not limited to, the information presented. For example, if you feel your classmate committed a great oversight, you have the opportunity to address your concern following the presentation.

Development of a Four-Week Course

Using what you would consider the most influential book read, students will develop a four-week course to teach the ideas/book to church members, family, or friends. The four-week plan should include:

1. An outline of how you would teach the content.
2. At least five discussion questions for each week.
3. At least three objectives to be accomplished during the four-week period.

Movie Reflection

Choose one movie from the provided list. Write a two-page summary and reflection of the movie.

1. Dawn Porter, Rick Bowers, et al., *Spies of Mississippi* (2014)
2. Douglas Blackmon, *Slavery by Another Name* (2012)
3. Spike Lee, *Do the Right Thing* (1989)
4. Toni Morrison, *Beloved* (1999)
5. Zora Neale Hurston, *Their Eyes Were Watching God* (2005)

Mandatory Course Readings

1. *A Knock at Midnight*, Martin Luther King Jr.
2. *African American Religions, 1500–2000 Colonialism, Democracy, and Freedom*, Sylvester Johnson

3. *Frederick Douglass: The Most Complete Collection of His Written Works and Speeches*, Frederick Douglass
4. *Phillis Wheatley: Complete Writings*, Phillis Wheatley
5. *The Autobiography of Malcolm X*, Alex Haley
6. *The Complete Poems of Paul Lawrence Dunbar*, Paul Lawrence Dunbar
7. *The Future of the American Negro*, Booker T. Washington
8. *The House I Live In: Race in the American Century*, Robert J. Norrell
9. *The Illusive Dream*, Korie L. Edwards
10. *The Miseducation of the Negro*, Carter G. Woodson
11. *The Souls of Black Folk*, W. E. B Du Bois
12. *Their Eyes Were Watching God*, Zora Neale Hurtson
13. *Why Are All the Black Kids Sitting Together in the Cafeteria?*, Beverly Daniel Tatum

Week	Reading	Lecture	
1	*The Miseducation of the Negro*	The mere imparting of wisdom is not education.	
2	*The Souls of Black Folk*	The double-aimed struggle of the black artisan	
3	*A Knock at Midnight*	King, the pastor	
4	*The House I Live In* **or** *African American Religions, 1500–2000 Colonialism, Democracy, and Freedom*	From the reconstruction to 2000. Race and racial construct.	Paper 1
5	*Why Are All the Black Kids Sitting Together in the Cafeteria?*	Is sitting together good or bad?	
6	*Phillis Wheatley*	A woman and slavery	
7	*The Future of the American Negro*	The constant struggle for freedom and moving forward	

8	Spring break or fall break inserted accordingly		Paper 2
9	*Their Eyes Were Watching God*	Is the struggle any different today?	
10	*The Autobiography of Malcolm X*	Malcolm, the man	
11	*The Autobiography of Malcolm X*	Malcolm and black pride	
12	*The Complete Poems of Paul Lawrence Dunbar* (reading through *On the Road*)	Blacks and poetical literature	Paper 3
13	*The Illusive Dream*	The struggle of constructing multiethnic churches	
14	*Frederick Douglass: The Most Complete Collection of His Written Works and Speeches*	The slave years	
15	*Frederick Douglass: The Most Complete Collection of His Written Works and Speeches*	The free years	Paper 4
16	*The Complete Poems of Paul Lawrence Dunbar* (second half of the collection)	Discussion of movies	

The rating system is as follows:

Rating	Grade	Rating	Grade
95–100	A+	60–64	B-
90–94	A	55–59	C+
85–89	A-	47–54	C
80–84	B+	40–46	C-
65–79	B	0–39	F

Classroom participation and feedback 10%

Critical essay presentation 10%

Movie reflection 10%

Development of four-week course 10%

Critical essays at 15 points each 60%

Disabilities

Note: If you have special needs that require accommodations, please see me immediately. I want each student in this course to succeed. Early identification of your needs allows us to help you more effectively.

University or Course Policy Regarding

On-campus or online academic resources

Late Work

Plagiarism

Style for Essays

Withdrawal from Course

BIBLIOGRAPHY

Books

Appleby, Joyce, Lynn Hunt, Margaret Jacob. *Telling the Truth About History*. New York: W. W. Norton, 1994.

Augustine. *On Christian Doctrine*. Pickerington: Beloved Publishing, 2014.

Bonhoeffer, Dietrich. *Life Together*. New York: Harper & Row, 1954.

Bordas, Juanas. *Salsa, Soul, and Spirit: Leadership for a Multicultural Age*. San Francisco: Berrett-Koehler, 2007.

Byron, Gay. *Symbolic Blackness and Ethnic Difference in Early Christian Literature: Blackened by Their Sins: Early Christian Ethno-Political Rhetorics About Egyptians, Ethiopians, Blacks, and Blackness*. London: Routledge, 2002.

Carter, Cameron J. *Race: A Theological Account*. New York: Oxford University Press, 2008.

DuPont, Carolyn R. *Mississippi Praying: Southern White Evangelicals and the Civil Rights Movement, 1945–1975*. New York: New York University Press, 2013.

Emerson, Michael, and Christian Smith, *Divided by Faith: Evangelical Religion and the Problem of Race in America*. New York: Oxford University Press, 2001.

Fanon, Frantz, *Black Skin, White Masks*, trans. Richard Philcox. New York: Grover Press, 1952.

Goen, C. C. *Broken Churches, Broken Nation*. Macon: Mercer University Press, 1997.

Harlow, Luke E. *Religion, Race, and the Making of Confederate Kentucky, 1830–1880*. New York: Cambridge University Press, 2014.

Harvey, Paul. *Redeeming the South: Religious Cultures and Racial Identities Among Southern Baptists, 1865–1925*. Chapel Hill: University of North Carolina Press, 1997.

Hays, Daniel J. *From Every People and Nation: A Biblical Theology of Race*. Downers Grove: InterVarsity Press, 2003.

Isaac, Benjamin. *The Invention of Racism in Classical Antiquity*. Princeton: Princeton University Press, 2004.

Kennedy, Rebecca F., C. Snydor Roy, and Max L. Goldman, eds. *Race and Ethnicity in the Classical World: An Anthology of Primary Sources in Translation*. Indianapolis: Hackett Publishing, 2013.

Kidd, Thomas S. and Barry Hankins, *Baptists in America: History*. New York: Oxford University Press, 2015.

Leonard, Bill J. *Baptists in America*. New York: Columbia University Press, 2005.

Mellon, James. *Bull Whip Days: The Slaves Remember—an Oral History*. New York: Grove Press, reprinted 2002.

Murray, Iain. *Revival and Revivalism: The Making and Marring of American Evangelicalism 1750–1858*. Carlisle: Banner of Truth, 1994.

Myrdal, Gunnar. *An American Dilemma: The Negro Problem and Modern Democracy, vol. 1*. New Brunswick: Transaction Publishers, 1995.

Ortman, Jennifer M., and Christine E. Guarneri, *United States Population Projections: 2000 to 2050*. Washington, DC: U.S. Census Bureau, 2014.

Pressler, Paul. *A Hill on Which to Die: One Southern Baptist's Journey*. Nashville: B&H, 2002.

Rahlfs, Albert, and Robert Hanhart. *Septuaginta*. Rev. Ed. Deutsche Bibelgesellschaft, 2007.

Sechrest, Love L. *A Former Jew: Paul and the Dialectics of Race*. London: T&T Clark, 2009.

Tucker, Brian J., and Coleman A. Baker, eds. *The T&T Clark Handbook to Social Identity in the New Testament*. New York: T&T Clark, 2014.

Williams, Jarvis J. *A Chosen Race and a Royal Priesthood: A Biblical Theology of Ethnic Identity*. Wheaton: Crossway, Forthcoming 2018.

———. *Commentary on Galatians*. New Covenant Commentary Series. Edited by Mike Bird and Craig Kenner. Eugene: Cascade Books, forthcoming 2018.

———. *For Whom Did Christ Die? The Extent of the Atonement in Paul's Theology*, Paternoster Biblical Monographs Series. Milton Keynes: Paternoster, 2012.

———. *One New Man: The Cross and Racial Reconciliation in Pauline Theology*. Nashville: B&H, 2010.

Wills, Gregory. *The Southern Baptist Theological Seminary, 1859–2009*. New York: Oxford University Press, 2009.

Yarshater, Eshan. *Encyclopaedia Iranica*. London: Routledge & Kegan Paul, 1996.

Essays

Becker, U. "Gospel," in *Dictionary of New Testament Theology*, 2:104–14. Edited by Collin Brown. Grand Rapids: Zondervan, 1986.

Smedley, Audrey. "Race," in *Oxford Companion to United States History*, 641–45. Oxford: Oxford University Press, 2001.

Articles

Gourley, Bruce. "John Leland: Evolving Views of Slavery, 1789–1839." *Baptist History and Heritage Journal*. 40:1 (Winter 2005), 104–16.

Storey, John W. "Thomas Buford Maston and the Growth of Social Christianity Among Texas Baptists." *East Texas Historical Journal*. 19:2, Article 7 (1981).

Newspaper Articles

Baptist, Edward E. "Teaching Slavery to Reluctant Listeners." *New York Times Sunday Magazine*. September 11, 2015.

Websites

Guinness World Records, "Largest Empire, by Percentage of World Population," in *Guinness Book of World Records*, http://www.guinnessworldrecords .com/world-records/largest-empire-by-percentage-of-world-population.

King, Martin Luther, Jr. "The Case Against 'Tokenism.'" *The New York Times*. August 5, 1962, accessed December 30, 2015, http://www.theking center.org/archive/document/new-york-times-case-against-tokenism#.

Baptist, Edward E. "Teaching Slavery to Reluctant Listeners." *The New York Times Magazine*. September 11, 2015, accessed July 26, 2016, http:// www.nytimes.com/2015/09/13/magazine/teaching-slavery-to-reluctant -listeners.html?_r=0.

Storey, John W. "Thomas Buford Maston and the Growth of Social Christianity Among Texas Baptists." *East Texas Historical Journal*. 19:2 (1981), accessed July 26, 2016, http://scholarworks.sfasu.edu/ethj /vol19/iss2/7.

Ortman, Jennifer M., Christine E. Guarneri. "United States Population Projections: 1000 to 2050." U.S. Census, accessed July 26, 2016, https:// www.census.gov/population/projections/files/analytical-document 09.pdf.

White, Randy. "I Don't Understand the Evangelical Response to Ferguson." Randy White Ministries, accessed July 26, 2016, http://www.randy-whiteministries.org/2014/11/26/dont-understand-evangelical-response -ferguson.

"Resolution on Colored Population." Southern Baptist Convention, accessed July 26, 2016, http://www.sbc.net/resolutions/31/resolution-on-colored-population.

Robinson, Jeff. "Pressler: Conservative Resurgence Was Grassroots Movement." Baptist Press, accessed July 26, 2016, http://www.bpnews.net/17956/pressler-conservative-resurgence-was-grassroots-movement.

http://live.sbc.net.s3-website-us-east-1.amazonaws.com/ondemand.html.

CONTRIBUTORS

Daniel L. Akin, president, Southeastern Baptist Theological Seminary

Mark A. Croston Sr., national director of black church partnerships, LifeWay Christian Resources

Matthew J. Hall, Dean of Boyce College of The Southern Baptist Theological Seminary

Toby Jennings, Instructor of Theology, Grand Canyon University and Seminary

Kevin M. Jones Sr., associate dean of academic innovation and assistant professor of teacher education, Boyce College of The Southern Baptist Theological Seminary

W. Dwight McKissic Sr., pastor, Cornerstone Baptist Church

Craig Mitchell, associate professor of philosophy, politics, and economics, Criswell College

R. Albert Mohler, Jr., president, The Southern Baptist Theological Seminary

Kevin L. Smith, executive director, the Baptist Convention of Maryland/ Delaware

Walter R. Strickland II, special advisor to the president for diversity and instructor of theology, Southeastern Baptist Theological Seminary

T. Vaughn Walker, senior pastor, First Gethsemane Baptist Church; Retired WMU professor of Christians ministries; and professor of black church studies, The Southern Baptist Theological Seminary

Jarvis J. Williams, associate professor of New Testament interpretation, The Southern Baptist Theological Seminary

K. Marshall Williams Sr., pastor, Nazarene Baptist Church

Curtis A. Woods, associate executive director for convention relations, Kentucky Baptist Convention

NAME INDEX

SCRIPTURE INDEX